First Steps in
Genealogy

A Beginner's Guide to
Researching Your Family History

Desmond Walls Allen

BETTERWAY BOOKS
CINCINNATI, OHIO

Other fine Betterway Books are available from your local bookstore or direct from the publisher.

02 01 00 99 98   5 4 3 2 1

Library of Congress Cataloging-in-Publication Data

Allen, Desmond Walls.
    First steps in genealogy : a beginner's guide to researching your family history / Desmond Walls Allen—1st ed.
        p.   cm.
    Includes bibliographical references (p. 138) and index.
    ISBN 1-55870-489-2 (pbk. : alk. paper)
    1. Genealogy. 2. United States—Genealogy—Handbooks, manuals, etc. I. Title.
CS16.A454   1998
929′.1—dc21   98-34129
                                                                          CIP

Production editor: Nicole R. Klungle
Interior designer: Mary Barnes Clark
Cover designer: Stephanie Redman
Cover illustrator: Brenda Grannan

The family group sheet reproduced on pages 34 and 35 and the pedigree chart appearing on page 38 are reprinted by permission of the Genealogy Records Service at http://www.genrecords.com. © 1998 Genealogy Records Service.

The family group sheet reproduced on page 36 and 37 is reprinted by permission of the Dallas Genealogical Society. © 1998 Dallas Genealogical Society.

About the Author

Desmond Walls Allen is the owner of Arkansas Research, a publishing company specializing in Arkansas records. She is a past president, life member, and member of the board of directors of the Arkansas Genealogical Society. She is cofounder and secretary-treasurer of Professional Genealogists of Arkansas, and editor of PGA's *Arkansas Historical and Genealogical Magazine.*

The genealogy columnist for the *Arkansas Democrat-Gazette* (Little Rock), she also contributes articles to *Heritage Quest* and *Ancestry* magazines.

Allen teaches and lectures at genealogical workshops and seminars throughout the nation, including National Genealogical Society (NGS) and Federation of Genealogical Societies (FGS) conferences. She also appeared in the PBS television ten-part series *Ancestors,* which aired in January 1997.

Allen served as trustee of the Association of Professional Genealogists from 1993 to 1994. She was awarded APG's Grahame Thomas Smallwood, Jr. Award of Merit in 1993; and she received the Federation of Genealogical Societies' Distinguished Service Award in 1994.

Acknowledgments

Martha Vaughn, aka Patsy the Witch

This photo of Patsy the Witch was taken around 1900 when Patsy was in her early nineties. A distant cousin of mine—also a descendant of Patsy—sent me the picture. Don't be afraid to contact relatives you only just discovered—they may want to share information as much as you do!

My ancestor, Martha "Patsy the Witch" Vaughn, deserves credit for my initial interest in genealogy. My great-grandmother told me about *her* great-grandmother, a woman who could predict the future, cast spells and change people into animals. Patsy the Witch dangles at the bottom of my pedigree chart—her line is my maternal one the whole way. I found her and *her* maternal grandmother as well.

This book wouldn't have been possible without the people from whom I learned research methods and all those students I, in turn, taught to do genealogy. The questions and stories from my students helped me decide what novice genealogists need to know. My special friend George's search for Grandma Jackson was a voyage of discovery for me, too.

Carolyn Earle Billingsley, my best friend and former business partner, was a great help in the creation of this book. She and I coauthored *Beginner's Guide to Family History Research*, the precursor to this volume. Leslie Smith Collier, a splendidly brilliant woman, made suggestions and recommendations that strengthened the book. My sister Henryetta Vanaman (an English major) was of tremendous help when I needed help on how to make a sentence read right.

Bill Brohaugh, my editor, was a joy and delight to work with.

And finally, my sincerest appreciation goes to my mother, Elizabeth O. Walls, for her unconditional love and encouragement. My son, Hadley Hirrill, was most supportive, especially when he learned my hours at the computer keyboard meant more discretionary money for him.

TABLE OF CONTENTS

INTRODUCTION

I wrote this book from a selfish standpoint, and I thought perhaps you'd like to know why. When I first started pursuing my family history, I thought of it as a search for *my* ancestors. Through the years, I discovered the people who turned up in my pedigree aren't just *my* ancestors—they're the ancestors of lots of folks. *My* ancestors may be *your* ancestors. And if you'll get busy and involve yourself in the research process, perhaps you'll solve some of the problems about *our* ancestors I haven't been able to.

I write a genealogy column for a newspaper, so I get lots of interesting mail. One researcher was positively alarmed about the number of his ancestors when he did the mathematical computation to learn how many ancestors were back there. He knew he had two parents, four grandparents, eight great-grandparents, and so on. So he took pencil in hand and started working out how many ancestors he was descended from in the one hundredth generation. (Go ahead, try this yourself. Your calculator won't handle the final results, so be prepared to do math the old-fashioned way.)

My correspondent got back to ten generations with his pencil and figured he was descended from 1,024 people in that generation. I can imagine a crowd of that size; you probably can, too. But when he reached twenty generations, he counted over a million people—slightly less than the current population of the entire state of Maine. If you don't get bogged down in the zeros, work back one hundred generations and you'll arrive at a number that boggles the mind. I had to use an encyclopedia to determine what numbers that large are called. The figure is 1,267,700,000,000,000,000,000,000,000,000. In layperson's terms, that's a little over 1.2 nonillion ancestors in the one hundredth generation.

The *Oxford American Dictionary* estimates a generation as thirty years. So one hundred generations would put us back to about 1000 B.C. Then we arrive at a problem—there weren't that many people on the earth. (And those were only *his* ancestors.) The population of the world in 1650 was only about five hundred million people.

Where had his thinking gone astray? He isn't descended from 1.2 nonillion *different* people who were exclusively *his* ancestors. He is the product of one hundred generations of intermarriage among the world's population. If you have New England ancestry, you'll probably discover many of your lines go back to just a few ancestral couples who came over in the seventeenth century. Their descendants intermarried.

The United States is a country on the move. We don't stay in the same location for dozens of generations like people of other countries did in historic (and prehistoric) times. So our pedigree charts are fairly diverse. But it isn't always so. In 1997, the news media ran stories about a man in an English village whose DNA matched that of a prehistoric skeleton. The stories said he was probably related to most of the people in the town.

And some of us whose ancestors left that town for America a couple of hundred years ago are probably related to that skeleton, too.

It's when we begin to see the big picture and think about all those ancestors of *ours* who wove the fabric of our pedigree that we realize we're all part of a global family. So, cousin, start on *your* family history research. Be sure to read "Step 10, Putting It All Together: Sharing Your Family History," page 126, because I want to know what you find out about *our* family.

WHERE'D YOU GET THOSE EYES?

The Why, What and How of Family History

Look in the mirror: Everything you see came from your ancestors—your eyes, the shape of your face, length of your nose, and a hundred other features. You inherited personality traits, disease predispositions and thousands of features you can't see. Who are you? You're the product of your ancestors' gene pool. Scary thought? Perhaps it's time for you to learn more about all those people who contributed to your makeup.

Why

Think about *why* you want to know about your ancestors.

Your interest in genealogy may come from ordinary curiosity about all the people who contributed to who you are. Genealogy research is not just about your ancestors—it's about self-discovery. You'll learn more about yourself when you hit the pedigree trail. If you're curious about your ancestors, you've probably reached the point in your life when you can turn inward. When people are young, they're often preoccupied with earning a living and rearing children. Somewhere in the growth process, your thoughts become introspective. You begin to want answers to questions such as, "Why am I like I am?"

Perhaps you have a medical problem and wonder if something in your genetic makeup contributed to the situation. You can learn who your ancestors were and attempt to discover their causes of death. We're reading more in the news about the importance of genetic research, and you may wonder where your genes came from and whether you may have inherited tendencies that leave you vulnerable to particular diseases.

Maybe you've heard family stories, legends and mysteries and want to learn more about them. With ongoing interest in the Civil War, you may want to find out who your ancestors were who served in that war. Or you might want to join a lineage society like the Daughters of the American Revolution or Mayflower Descendants. If you're descended from or related to a famous ancestor, your research may take you in that direction.

Your interest may not be from self-interest at all. Perhaps you want to help someone with a school project. Social studies teachers often assign genealogical projects. Or you may want to do some research about someone else's family as a gift or reward. Perhaps your grandmother-in-law is in failing health and needs someone to do her "legwork" on her genealogy research. Or possibly you're going on vacation to an area where your neighbors' ancestors lived, and they want you to "just drop into the courthouse" for them.

Whatever your motivation, you'll be hooked on this hobby once you experience a little success. And that's what this book is about—your success.

What

What do you want to know? If you start on your search expecting to find only positive things about your ancestors, you may be in for a surprise. Ancestors have an odd habit of being human.

Do you just want to know the names of your ancestors? Will a pedigree chart listing your direct ancestors be enough to satisfy your curiosity?

Probably you'll want to learn as much as you can about all your ancestors as far back in time as possible. And you'll want to know about your *entire* family; those atrocious aunts, colorful cousins and unique uncles can add spice to your family history.

How

You know *why* you want to know, and you know *what* you want to know. Now let's take care of *how* you'll find out. This book is designed to set you on the right path to begin your genealogical research. It isn't the only book you'll need on the subject, and it doesn't contain *everything* you'll need to know. But it will get you headed in the right direction.

Keep two concepts in mind as you wade into the research process:
- *How* you know is as important as *what* you know.
- Your search isn't just about *names*, it's about *people*.

From the beginning, keep track of the sources of your information—you'll be glad you did later on. Genealogy isn't just about collecting information; it's about analyzing and evaluating what you find. And to do that, you have to know where your information came from.

With all of today's databases of names, it's possible to lose sight of your objective and turn genealogy into a search for names. Your ancestors were much more than names—they were living, breathing human beings who were born, interacted with other people, and died. They didn't exist in a vacuum—they were part of a community, part of larger groups of people.

First we need to talk about what traits will make you a good genealogical researcher. It's helpful to be adventurous, analytical, consistent, courteous, creative, curious, determined, patient, skeptical and well organized. If this description doesn't completely fit you now, it's still possible for you to become a very good genealogist, but you may have to develop some of these traits along the way.

The place to begin is with yourself. Your search for ancestors is about yourself. You may want to keep a journal or write your autobiography. Begin your search for information in your home. Raid the refrigerator for those stories that have been in cold storage all these years. Visit family cemeteries.

Before you overwhelm yourself with information, organize your facts. Correspondence, traditional and electronic, may become a big part of your routine.

The reference librarian might become your new best friend. Your search will take you to libraries and archives. You'll look for previously published books and articles about your family lines, and search for newly found cousins who may be working on the ancestors you have in common with them. When you run out of these sources, you're on your own to look for more information that can help you piece together your pedigree.

Bread and butter, Fred Astaire and Ginger Rogers, history and genealogy; some things just go together. In order to understand your ancestors, you can learn about the times in which they lived. The political, social, economic and geographic history of the time and place in which they lived can give you insights into what they did and why they did it.

Then we'll dive into federal census records, a mainstay of genealogical research. Imagine a nationwide photo—the federal government took one every ten years. The other most-used records for genealogists come from courthouses where your ancestors went to do their day-to-day business. You'll learn how to access census and courthouse records.

After you've accumulated information, evaluated it, analyzed what it means and organized it, you'll probably want to share what you've learned with other members of your family. You can rally your cousins and stage a family reunion. Perhaps you'll join genealogical societies, or create a home page on the Internet.

At the end of this book, you'll find a Resources section (Appendix B) that will help you find forms, books and other useful information. The Guide for Source Citation (Appendix A) gives you examples to follow.

The important fact is you've begun your search for your family history by picking up this book. You've taken the first step! In the following chapters, you'll learn about starting a successful genealogical search.

STEP 2

PLAYING SHERLOCK HOLMES
The Genealogist's Skills and Goals

Before you start your search for ancestors, let's examine your skills. You're motivated to start your quest for ancestors; after all, you've picked up this book. There are some skills that can assist your research. You probably already have most of them.

Here's a hint—and keep this in mind as you read through this chapter. If you're great at research, but not good at organization or correspondence, then enlist the aid of one of your siblings, or your spouse or a cousin. If you love corresponding with people, but don't enjoy the tedious work at the microfilm reader, use the buddy system to get the work done. Team up with someone who is good at the things you aren't.

Helpful Skills

Inquisitiveness

Sherlock Holmes would have made a good genealogist. A keen, inquiring mind and a sense of adventure are essential. As you learn more from interviews, records and reading, always ask "Why?" and think about where new information will lead. Don't stop with a single document—follow the tracks it leaves. A death certificate may take you to funeral home records, newspaper obituaries, census schedules, military service and pension records, employment records, marriage licenses, probate court documents and more.

Critical Thinking

Critical thinking skills are essential. You must learn to question the validity of the sources you uncover. Is the death certificate correct? Does it match other known facts? Who gave the information that appears on the document? Is that person likely to be biased or have a reason for giving incorrect information? Even published family histories you find about your ancestors may not be accurate. Just because something is in print doesn't make it so, and you must learn to evaluate the accuracy of the stories you hear and records you find.

Organizational Ability

Organizational skills are very helpful to a genealogist. You might be a great detective and locate all kinds of information, but you must be able to organize the materials you find both physically and in your mind. Good record-keeping skills will help you pursue genealogy. The ability to take notes and write summaries of your research results will help you tremendously.

Avid Reading

Avid readers make better family historians. All the reading you've done of everything from history books to mystery novels will increase your understanding in your search. And to learn more about successful research methods, you need to read books and articles about how to find your ancestors. But then, you are already taking the first step in that direction, aren't you?

Listening

Developing the art of listening can do wonders for your genealogy. Listen to reference librarians, more experienced genealogists and your older relatives. Some people ask a question, then concentrate on formulating their next question instead of listening to the answer to their original question. Digest answers. Listen for nuances of meaning. If your great-aunt hesitates when you ask about Grandma's first marriage, is it because she doesn't remember the details, or is it because she's deciding how *much* she should tell you about it? Give her a minute; look expectant. Don't speak just to fill the silence. Really listen with your whole body.

Listen to documents, too. Don't just read a marriage record and copy the facts from it. Listen to it. The record is saying two people decided to take a momentous step in their lives. Why did they do it? Who were the family and friends who supported their decision? Where did the marriage take place? Was there a celebration after the ceremony? Where did they plan to live? Listen to documents.

Consistency

Consistency is a good thing for genealogists. Take dates, for example. How many ways can you write your birthdate? July 25, 1950; 07/25/50;

25 July 1950; the twenty-fifth of July, nineteen hundred and fifty; 7.25.50; 19500725; 25/7/50. And these are just some of the possibilities. In genealogical circles, the "standard" format for writing a date is 25 July 1950, what some folks refer to as "military style." The day of the month comes first, followed by the month spelled as a word, then the year as a *four*-digit number.

There are exceptions to this practice. If you're copying dates from a written or published source, don't change the format—copy them just as you find them. One genealogist painstakingly transcribed old Quaker (Society of Friends) records and changed the dates she found there to the standard genealogical format. Dates in the record were expressed in the form "3.1.1742." Later, she found that Quakers, like other English groups, started their year with March as the first month.

Be consistent not only with dates, but with number formats, name conventions and your note taking. If you consistently write the citation for your source in your notes *before* you examine it, you'll be much less likely to come away from a library with a sheet of notes from some unknown book and wonder later where it came from. If you consistently copy names just as you find them, even when they're abbreviated, you won't wonder later whether the name was actually "Joseph" in the record and you were in a hurry and jotted down "Jos." or whether the name was "Jos." in the record.

Skepticism

A healthy dose of skepticism is good for any genealogist. Just because Aunt Mozelle says it, doesn't make it so. If you hear a tale about your family's descent from royalty, or a missed opportunity for a fabulous fortune or something else that sounds a bit fantastic, reserve judgment about it and search for corroborating evidence.

Skepticism is one of those traits that defines your level as a researcher. As a beginner, you tend to believe everything you're told, even the bizarre stories. "Grandma lived to be 115 years old"—that sort of thing. After you progress a bit and develop a little skepticism, you learn to interpret that as "Grandma probably lived to be very old." But do write down everything you're told, no matter how incredible it seems. And note who told you or where you read it. You'll probably find some grain of truth in the tale.

Courtesy

Courtesy goes a long way in genealogical pursuits. The old adage, "You can catch more flies with honey than with vinegar," applies to catching ancestors as well. Librarians, record custodians and other people in public positions respond positively to smiles and expressions of appreciation. Your relatives will, too.

Patience

Patience will make your search more enjoyable. It's hard to wait for the reply to a letter. If the clerk only knew how important that marriage record is to you, perhaps she'd hurry! You want to know who your ancestors were and you want to know *now*. Practice a little patience. If you don't receive a response to an inquiry after a month of applied patience, then you can write again, asking if perhaps your letter was mislaid. Some libraries and agencies routinely take a long time to respond. The New York vital records office often takes nine months to send a death certificate.

Creativity

Be creative. Do try conventional methods first, but be open to unusual ideas. Use your personal frame of reference. You know your life is involved with groups of people; your ancestors' lives were, too. You may belong to labor organizations, business groups, religious bodies, trade unions, retired military associations, college fraternities or sororities, social clubs, softball teams, bowling leagues, Elvis fan clubs or any of hundreds of others. Your ancestors were part of groups, too. They interacted with other people, and the records on those folks may help you find your family.

Vision

Think expansively. Being able to see the "big picture" will help you find your ancestors. You're probably part of a large family, even if you're an only child, when you include your spouse's relatives, ex-spouse's relatives, first cousins, aunts and uncles and grandparents. Your extended family may include your brother-in-law's parents and family. Or the family of your grandmother's second husband. Your ancestors were part of interconnected family alliances, too. You'll have better chances for success in finding that elusive place of previous residence if you follow a group of people backward in time instead of a single family.

Extroversion

Be an extrovert. After you've done genealogical research for a while, you'll realize we're all part of one big worldwide family. Potential cousins are everywhere. Develop an interest in other people's genealogy. In the chapter on courthouse research, you're cautioned not to bore the county clerk or the staff with stories about *your* ancestors. But it doesn't hurt to ask about *their* ancestors. One researcher asked a deputy clerk about her ancestors and learned they shared a great-great-grandmother.

CREATIVE METHODS PAY OFF

George began his search for his ancestors with only a little family information. He knew his mother, Zeffie, had been reared by her maternal grandmother, a woman known to the family simply as "Grandma Jackson." Her first name was lost to George's generation and his mother had died years before. He knew Grandma Jackson had lived in western Arkansas, and the only remarkable thing he could remember from relatives' tales was that she had twins named "Lige" and "Bige." It wasn't much to go on.

Zeffie's mother, Alice, had died shortly after the birth of her third child, and the three children had been deserted by their father, Walter Owens, and left in the care of Grandma Jackson. Some simple guesswork and math pinpointed the time period in question as around the turn of the century, because George's mother was born in 1899. George's older sisters remembered that their mother's childhood, but not her teen years, had been spent with her grandmother.

A trip to the library and a search of the 1910 federal census schedules for Arkansas turned up the three Owens children in the home of an uncle, Sam Jackson. But no Grandma Jackson. The search in the census was aided by a statewide "Soundex" index, a system that groups like-sounding last names together under numerical code numbers, then organizes them alphabetically by the first name of the head of the household. (For further discussion of Soundex indexes, see pages 93-97.)

Figuring that Grandma Jackson must have died before the census was taken in 1910, a search in the old newspaper issues on microfilm was George's next step. Reading the newspapers told him a lot about the community in which his

family had lived. It also turned up a 1909 obituary for Grandma Jackson. The story in the paper told about her character, her death, the final illness, and described her funeral right down to the names of the songs that were sung. But she was referred to only as "Grandma" Jackson. An obituary in a newspaper published in a neighboring town mentioned that her burial had taken place in Blackfork Cemetery.

A search of all the Jackson households listed in the 1900 Soundex index for Arkansas was tedious, but it paid off when George found the listing for a Margaret Jackson in a western Arkansas county. She had twin sons in her home listed as "Elijah" and "Abijah." They had to be Lige and Bige. Grandma had a first name at last.

It was time for a field trip. George called the funeral home in the county seat of Polk County, Grandma Jackson's place of residence, to learn the location of Blackfork Cemetery. The cemetery was small and located in a remote area. But it was well cared for. George examined every gravestone, but didn't find one for Grandma Jackson. He found names of Grandma Jackson's neighbors he recognized from the census microfilm. He even found one for a Jackson child that must have belonged to one of Grandma's sons. But no Grandma.

Discouraged, scratched by briars, and bitten by chiggers, he was ready to give up. Then he had a creative idea. He wrote a note asking anyone with information about Grandma Jackson's grave to please call him, and he left the card with his name and phone number in a sandwich bag tied to the cemetery's gatepost. He was confident, since the cemetery was obviously mowed on a regular basis, that people still cared about the graves there. He hoped the cemetery caretaker or other visitors might know where Grandma was buried.

Months went by before the cemetery caretaker called. She didn't know where Grandma Jackson was buried, but she supplied the name of a Jackson relative who might know. That led George to a previously unknown cousin from Oklahoma who had been present at Grandma Jackson's burial. Though only a child at the time, she remembered where her grandmother had been buried. She agreed to meet George at the cemetery and show

him the grave. The grave was marked, but only with a large rock, not a tombstone. George later arranged to have a large marble gravestone erected for her. Grandma Jackson—found at last, thanks to a creative step in genealogical research.

Postscript: George didn't stop with Grandma, of course. He followed the Jackson family back into colonial North Carolina. Grandma Jackson's maternal line, the Hunter family, took him to seventeenth-century Virginia. Newly discovered cousins shared photographs, not only of Grandma Jackson, but of long-forgotten Grandpa Jackson as well.

Is This You?

Do you have any or all of these traits and skills that are helpful to genealogists? Are you an adventurous person with an inquiring mind? Are you an organized, consistent person who reads a lot and applies critical-thinking skills? Are you a patient, courteous person who listens well? Are you a creative extrovert who sees the big picture? You'll make an excellent genealogist. If this description doesn't fit you, remember that you can learn these skills and acquire these traits. And you can team up with a fellow researcher whose personality and abilities complement yours.

Linking Generations

Genealogy isn't just about finding your *ancestors*. You must find those *records* connecting each generation to parents in previous generations. One misstep in making those links may send you off on someone else's family line.

Genealogy isn't an exact science. Today, we have DNA testing methods that can definitively establish parentage. But when we get past our living parents and grandparents, DNA testing is not practical and, for the most part, not possible. When we run out of living relatives, we have to rely on records. And the information we find in those records can be confusing, misleading or just plain wrong.

So we have to evaluate all the data we find. And we're obligated to look for *all* the records about a particular subject, not just the ones that are easy to find or the ones that say what we want to believe. Then we must analyze the information we've found in our sources and interpret what we've found.

GENEALOGY IS ABOUT PEOPLE

Nancy had been curious about her family history for a long time, but she was a busy elementary school teacher and didn't have time to do any serious research until she retired. She knew the man she'd called "daddy" was her stepfather, and that she came from her mother's first marriage. Her stepfather had been a wonderful man, and she'd always hesitated to ask questions about her biological father, because she didn't want her "daddy" to think there was something lacking in their relationship. Her stepfather had died by the time Nancy retired, and she decided she would ask her mother about her "real" father. But Nancy's mother was unwilling to discuss her first marriage.

Without her mother's help, Nancy started her search based on the information from her birth certificate. That document gave her father's name as John Underwood and his birthplace as Illinois. She knew from looking at her mother's scrapbooks that the couple had been members of a traveling group of theatrical performers during the late 1920s when tent shows featuring dramatic plays were as popular as movies are today. Nancy found a marriage record for her parents and learned from a newspaper clipping they'd been married in a newspaper office in one of the towns where their troupe was performing. The marriage had helped generate some publicity for the show. She also found a divorce record for the couple filed not long after her birth.

With the information she'd discovered, Nancy asked volunteers in the local genealogy group for help in locating her father in the federal census schedules for 1920, the most recent available to researchers. She was able to find Underwood in the 1910 and 1900 census records.

Urged by her friends in the genealogy group, Nancy approached her mother with the information she'd found in the records about her father's family. Faced with Nancy's continued interest in family history, her mother revealed that Underwood wasn't Nancy's father at all. She had been married to Underwood, but had had an affair with another man while Underwood was employed with a different group of actors.

Nancy's mother told her who her true biological father was. Then Nancy remembered visits during her childhood from an Aunt Jewel and Uncle Dave, though she never knew her exact relationship to them. Her mother told her Uncle Dave was her father and Aunt Jewel was Dave's sister. They had stayed in touch with Nancy's mother until Nancy was a young married woman.

Nancy searched for more information and found Dave and Jewel were both deceased. Dave had married several years after Nancy's birth and had two children. Nancy was able to find them and developed a rewarding, ongoing relationship with her newly found half sister, Jerri. Jerri shared photos and stories with Nancy about their father and gave her a volume of poetry and a painting created by him. Nancy was later able to research her real father's family lines through traditional written records.

Nancy's voyage into family history took her into some rough seas. She was able to get on the right track because she maintained her curiosity, but at the same time respected her mother's feelings and didn't press her for information. After the breakthrough, Nancy's mother seemed relieved to be able to talk about her past. She and Nancy grew closer through the experience.

Even then, we may be wrong. Genealogy is about people, and sometimes they behave just like human beings, not subjects in a scientific study. The father in a record may not be the biological father. Sometimes we find information that concerns, shocks, dismays or embarrasses us. It's all part of our family's history. We can't change it; we just have to accept what we find and continue our search one generation at a time.

Research Reports

To prove the links between generations, we always hope to find documents that say Robert was the father of John. Modern vital records supply that kind of certainty. Wills, deeds and court records that specifically mention relationships establish the links we're seeking. But sometimes we aren't lucky enough to find such straightforward sources. Then we have to gather all the information that exists about a particular family and attempt to interpret and analyze what we've found and make the best possible decision about whether Robert could be the father of John.

As you accumulate, interpret and analyze information about a family, it may become clear—to you, anyway—who the parents of an individual must have been. But it isn't enough just to *know* it; you must be able to tell others why you think so.

Put your thought processes in writing—think of it as a "thought experiment." List the pieces of evidence you've found and what they mean. List, as well, the sources you knew about but didn't have access to and couldn't search. List the sources you searched that didn't produce any information. Use the citation guide in Appendix A to be sure you give complete information about your sources.

Argue with yourself on paper; say what else the evidence could mean. Write about any evidence that points to a contrary possibility. If you're disagreeing with a written book or article, be sure to give a complete citation to the material.

Then write your conclusion. Your conclusion may be that you don't have enough information to make a decision about the point in question.

Title these written thoughts as a "research report." Put the name of the family at the top of the report and add your name and address as "prepared by." Date the report. Why would you put all this on a report to yourself? Because the report may find a wider audience some day, outside your files. The cousin you share it with may fax or mail it to half the known world (well, the ones working on your family, anyway).

When you write this kind of report, you're helping yourself clarify your thoughts by putting them in written form. You're writing a reminder of sorts to yourself about the progress of your research. You may have to lay your work aside for a period of time, either until you can obtain access to the additional resources you need or until you have time to return to your research.

RESEARCH REPORT ON ANDREW COLLET (1784-1863) ————— *Family name*

Was He a Son to Isaac Collet ————— *Topic of the report*
of Greene County, Tennessee?

Date your report.

DATE: 3 July 1997

PREPARED BY:
Gene E. Alogist ————— *Researcher's name and address*
1956 Anystreet
Anytown, OH 12345

————— *A brief summary of the question*

Proof exists that the records of Andrew Collet in Greene and Campbell Counties, Tennessee, and Cole County, Missouri, are all the same man. The argument for including Andrew as a son to the Isaac Collet family hinges on two documents: the sale of the estate of Isaac Collet and a deed in Greene County in which James Pebley sells his land to Abraham Collet. The first establishes that Isaac Collet likely left an heir named Andrew; the second links Andrew Collet to both Abraham Collet and James Pebley, who had moved from Greene County to Campbell County. There are multiple reasons for the assumption that the Andrew Collet of Campbell County is the Andrew Collet of Cole County, Missouri.

This researcher has listed all the small questions she had to answer before coming to a conclusion—a good way to stay organized!

Was Andrew Collet of Cole County, Missouri, the same man earlier seen in Campbell County, Tennessee?

1. Andrew's 1850 and 1860 Census listings in Cole County, Missouri, assert birth in Tennessee about 1784. (1850, Cole County, p. 55; 1860, Cole County, p. 227)

Evidence ———
2. Andrew purchased property in Cole County, Missouri, by 1838. (Ford, *History of Cole, Moniteau, Morgan, Benton, Miller, Maries and Osage Counties,* ————— *Source* *Missouri* [Easley, SC: Southern Historical Press, 1978], p. 213) No man of this name lived in Missouri in the 1830 Census; only one appeared in Missouri in the 1840 Census. (Cole County, page 71)

3. Only one man named Andrew Collet was on the 1830 Census of Tennessee, in Campbell County, page 228. That man is not seen in Tennessee in the 1840 Census.

4. The identified children of Andrew who were living at the time of the 1850 Census all show Tennessee births: Isaac Collet, born about 1811; Sarah Collet Smith (wife of Ali Smith), born 1822.

Evidence ———
5. Andrew's younger identified son, Anderson Collet, served in the Mexican War in a unit formed in Campbell County, Tennessee. (National Archives film ————— *Source* series M629, roll 8, "Index to compiled Service Records of Volunteer Soldiers Who Served During Indian Wars and Disturbances, 1815-58") He died in Cole County, Missouri, in 1845. (Cole Co., MO, Probate packet 113A-4; entered probate 14 October 1845)

Page 1 of 2 ————— *Number your pages to keep them together.*

Figure 2-1: Research Report The genealogist who prepared this report had researched one branch of her family back to a man named Andrew Collet. However, she could not find any direct evidence—such as a birth certificate— of Andrew's parentage or birthplace. After some research, she thought she knew who Andrew's father was, so she took the next step: writing a research report. She wrote out a statement of the question, and listed evidence and cited documents that supported her conclusion. Reproduced here are excerpts from her final research report.

Prepared by: Gene E. Alogist

Put your name and the date on each page of your report.

3 July 1997

Was Andrew Collet of Campbell County, TN, the same seen earlier in Greene County, TN?

1. Never from 1810 through 1830 do two men named Andrew Collet appear anywhere in the state. A man of this name left records in Greene County through the tax records of 1818, then appeared in the records of Campbell County in 1820, after which time he never again appeared in records of Greene County.

Evidence

2. There is a deed in Greene County made 17 December 1816 in which James Pebley, then of Campbell County, sells his Greene County property to Abraham Collet of Greene County. This deed was witnessed by Andrew and John Collet. The deed was not proven and recorded until 1825, at which time only John Collet appeared to prove the document. This suggests that Andrew Collet was no longer available in Greene County to swear the deed and also provides a definite link between these localities. (Greene County Deed Book 12, p. 321) — *Source*

3. Andrew Collet was witness to the will made 17 August 1833 in Campbell County by neighbor Charles Bratcher, a name that earlier occurred in Greene County. (Campbell County Will Book 1, p. 303)

Conclusion ——— *The conclusion contains a summary of the evidence and the results of the research.*

Yes, Andrew Collet of Cole County, Missouri is the same man found earlier in Campbell County, Tennessee, and even earlier in Greene County, Tennessee. In that locality only Isaac Collet is a potential father, for he is the only man of the correct name and anywhere near the correct age. Isaac's probate consists of the naming of an administrator (which Andrew is not), and the report of the sale of Isaac's worldly goods. At this estate sale, Andrew Collett is the most prominent purchaser. He also names his first son ''Isaac'' and sustains numerous, long-running associations with other men claimed as sons to Isaac. Andrew Collet _is_ a son to Isaac Collet of Greene County, Tennessee, even though Andrew is noticeably omitted from the Washington County, Tennessee, modern family history book.

For further study ——— *This researcher has listed some ideas for further investigation!*

Theopolis Miller also bought very heavily at the sale of Isaac Collet. He is the only man whose surname is not Collet who took a share of crops. It is certainly possible that the wife of Theopolis is either Isaac's widow or an older Collet daughter. Pursue it--this family could use some girlish influence!

Search the records of neighboring Jefferson County as well, for Isaac Collet sold land there not long before his death . . . might turn up new views.

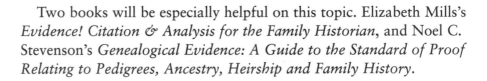

Two books will be especially helpful on this topic. Elizabeth Mills's *Evidence! Citation & Analysis for the Family Historian*, and Noel C. Stevenson's *Genealogical Evidence: A Guide to the Standard of Proof Relating to Pedigrees, Ancestry, Heirship and Family History.*

Citing Sources

We can't interpret, analyze or formulate conclusions if we don't know where our information came from. So you have to say how you know what you know. *How* you know is as important as *what* you know. So start now, while you're a beginner to genealogy, and carefully note where you get each piece of information. Do this as you find data.

If your source is a printed volume, gather all the elements about the book just as you did when you were writing a high school term paper: title, author, publisher, and the year and place of publication. Don't worry about the order of these elements; never mind where the commas and periods go. Just be sure to make a note about them on the photocopies or notes you take from the book. Add another item: a reminder to yourself about the library or archive where you found the book. Many genealogy books are printed in small press runs, and some future researcher may wonder where a copy of the book is located. (The reminder may be helpful to you, as well.)

Do the same thing for magazine, newsletter, newspaper and journal articles. Record the author, article title, periodical name, volume and issue and the date of publication.

Information you find on microfilm is actually published information, and you should record the same kind of information as for other published sources, but you'll add the microfilm roll number and any other identifying information. Federal census schedules are most often found as microfilmed copies of the originals, and they're actually publications of the National Archives in Washington, DC.

Many genealogical sources are now being published on CD-ROM. You can cite this kind of record just as you would a book—author or compiler, title of the CD-ROM, publisher, and date and place of publication.

The source you use for information may never have been published. It may be a letter, diary, public record, gravestone, church record or even an E-mail message. In general, say who wrote it, what it is, where it is now, and give enough information so someone unfamiliar with your research could find that document or object again. Add notes about the condition of the item, or any special circumstances that impact your evaluation and analysis of it.

Sometimes it's difficult to decide whether a source is published or not. In general, if copies of it have been distributed, especially for commercial purposes, it's a published record. Some people say Web pages posted on the Internet are published records—they're there for public consumption.

A simple guide for basic source citation is included in Appendix A. The examples show you the elements of information you need to write a citation for many of the common kinds of documents genealogists use as evidence.

You may hear the argument from time to time that keeping up with sources is too time-consuming and too much trouble. It isn't *fun*, like finding new information about your ancestors. Without that source information, though, you can't evaluate what you've found. You can't analyze the information and draw conclusions. And you can't pass on what you've learned, because the cousin to whom you pass along your information is going to ask, "But how do you *know*?"

Come on, Sherlock, gather your toolbox of skills and get ready to begin. Let's learn where to start your genealogical research.

STEP 3

BEGINNING AT THE BEGINNING

Your Family History *Starts* With You

Start your genealogy project with yourself. After all, when you started reading this book, you looked in the mirror, didn't you? (Because you wondered where you got those eyes.)

Proving Who *You* Are

Your genealogical research starts with *you*. Begin by examining your birth certificate. You'll probably be surprised at the amount of information it contains. Depending upon the place and time period it was issued, it probably lists:

- your full name at birth
- your sex and whether or not you were part of a multiple birth
- date of birth
- county and state of birth
- usual residence of your mother
- mother's full maiden name
- her age and race
- state or foreign country of her birth
- number of her previous children
- number of her living children
- father's full name
- his age and race
- state or foreign country of his birth
- his usual occupation
- kind of business or industry in which he worked
- name of the informant
- attending physician or midwife's name

- signature of the doctor or midwife
- name of the hospital or institution
- date of registration
- registration numbers of the certificate
- and usually the certification by the state registrar attesting that it is a true and correct copy of the record

If you don't already have a copy of your birth certificate, you can request one from the state bureau of vital records in the state where you were born. You've probably had to produce this document at some other time in your life—when you entered school, applied for a Social Security card, or had some other reason to prove who you are.

If your parents are alive, question them about the circumstances of your birth. Where did your family live when you were born? Is the house still there? Have you been back to visit? If your parents are deceased, perhaps you can question an older brother or sister, or one of your aunts or uncles.

School records may supply information about you. Not only the course of study, but family information is probably listed in them as well. You may remember the names of the schools you attended. Write to them and request copies of your records. If the school no longer exists, the state department of education may help you learn what happened to the records.

If you're a member of a religious group, there are probably records in their files that contain personal information about you, and if you've been a member since childhood, the names of your parents may be a part of their records.

When you begin your search for information about yourself, look for scrapbooks and photo albums. Perhaps your parents kept a baby book for you with copies of your birth announcement and newspaper clippings about your birth.

If you're adopted, you have *two* sets of parents, one who chose you, the other biological. You're a part of your adoptive family, so you can research those family lines as well as those of your natural parents. Because of the secrecy usually involved in an adoption, it's frequently difficult to determine the identities of the natural parents. And because there was a break in the handing down of family traditions, adopted people sometimes face a tough research situation. The situation isn't hopeless; it just takes more work and some time to learn about adoption research. *The Adoption Searchbook: Techniques for Tracing People* by Mary Jo Rillera is an example of the kind of book that can help with adoption research.

Make a list of the places you lived as a child. Try to remember the street addresses. If you can't remember the exact dates of moves your family made, correlate them with your school experience. Did you move between fifth and sixth grade? Ask older brothers and sisters for help.

Can you compile a list of all the jobs you've had? Construct a list just as though you were composing a résumé.

Write to the Social Security Administration (the address is in the Resources section, Appendix B, of this book) and request a copy of the SS-5 form you filled out to get your Social Security card. You probably requested one when you were about to get your first job. The SS-5 asked for information about yourself and your parents, including your mother's maiden name and the birthplaces of your parents. How much did you know then? You may be surprised about what you wrote on the form.

Look at the amount of information that exists to document *your* life. See how much information is available about *you*?

Organize all this information, keeping the important papers and discarding only those that you know are not important. If you have doubts about whether to keep or toss an item, keep it. (Yes, it *is* difficult for anyone with a genealogical tendency to throw away records.) By keeping what's important and winnowing your files, you'll make it easier for some genealogist in the future to learn about you.

Writing About Yourself

Gather all the information you've found about yourself and consider writing your autobiography. Record your life story so your descendants can learn more about you when they begin their search for ancestors. Writing about your life will cause you to reflect upon it. Think of it as a prelude to your journal about your genealogical quest. For more information about writing your life story, see Ruth Kanin's *Write the Story of Your Life*.

If you aren't quite ready for the autobiography project, begin writing in small segments about interesting events in your life. Keep a journal. You can keep a journal of your day-to-day life. Write about the little things. Record your thoughts and feelings. Keep writing, and someday you'll have some raw material for your autobiography. The journal itself will have value to your descendants.

Keep the journal in whatever format is easiest for you. If you want to handwrite it, why not buy a lovely blank book to inspire your thoughts? Maybe loose-leaf is a better idea if you write, then rewrite. If you're accustomed to typing your thoughts, keep an electronic journal. But do take time to store hard-copy, paper printouts of your journal.

Keeping a journal can lift your spirits. When something especially wonderful happens, write about it and capture your feelings. Reread your journal entries from time to time, especially the uplifting parts.

Your search for your ancestors is like starting on a journey of discovery. Why not keep a journal about your experiences in finding your roots? Record more than just the places you went to do research and what you found. Express how you felt when you first found your grandparents on a federal census schedule, or learned the names of grandparents you didn't know before you started. Describe the faces of those new cousins you met through a common interest in genealogy. Do they look like you?

Genealogy research isn't just about your ancestors—it's about *you*, too. The journey of discovery isn't just about finding ancestors, it's about finding out who *you* are. After you've found records about yourself, it's time to expand your research into home and family sources about your parents.

RAIDING THE REFRIGERATOR
Searching Home Sources for Information

It's time to remember the family stories, pull out the family photos, and gather the family papers that have been sitting around for years, waiting for someone to discover them. Your genealogical search begins at home. You started by gathering information about yourself and your life. Now it's time to expand your search and find information about your family members.

Family Stories

Family stories can be a wonderful part of your family history. Most families have some family legends that have been handed down. Most are verbal tales, no one ever wrote them on paper. It's difficult to recall all the stories you've heard. Some of the details will escape you. When you think of a story, write as much of it as possible.

Perhaps you heard family stories when you were a child. Grandpa may have told tales about his grandfather riding with the Jesse James outlaw gang. There may be a family story about the immigrant ancestor who left the "old" country to make a new life in America. Perhaps your grandmother remembers moving to California during the Great Depression of the 1930s.

Write the stories now! Put them on paper before they fade away. Family legends have a way of changing through time as they're told and retold. Everyone remembers them a bit differently. Seek out your older relatives and ask for their versions of the family stories. Don't add their versions to yours, write them separately and be sure to make a notation about who told you, and when and where you heard it.

Consider making an audio- or videotape recording of your relatives telling family stories. Ask older relatives about any bits of family information they remember. When did Uncle Charlie die? Was it before or after Cousin Clyde left for the Korean War? Ask about places, too. *Where* was Uncle Charlie buried?

Place names are very important in genealogy because public records are kept according to jurisdiction which is usually based on geographic areas. Any clues your living relatives can supply about previous places of residence for family members will help you when your research turns to public records.

When you ask family members for information, they can't always supply exact dates, but they can often bracket the event. If Uncle Charlie died before Cousin Clyde left for the Korean War, was it before or after Great-grandmother's death in 1947? If the family member remembers Great-grandma being at Uncle Charlie's funeral, it was before 1947. Be careful, though. One researcher learned her ancestor died during "the year of the big flood." The river was too high for some members of the family to attend the funeral, her cousin remembered. Much has been written about the Flood of 1927, but a search for a newspaper obituary was fruitless. With more questions, she learned there was also a "big flood" in 1923. And that, the newspapers confirmed, was the year the ancestor died.

The best way to learn about interviewing techniques is to actually interview your relatives. Practice on close family members who'll forgive you for fumbling with the audio or video recorder and asking dumb questions. Sometimes, for the relatives you're around frequently, you don't need to conduct formal interviews to gather information—just be alert for clues about the past in your conversations.

In an interview, you're trying to learn your subject's story. It isn't a criminal interrogation or a legal deposition. Ask permission, then set up the interview for a specific place and time. Give your interviewee some advance notice about what you want to know. If you have them, you can take along photos, heirlooms or documents to jump start the person's memory.

Don't tire your subject, and be sure *you* aren't doing all the talking. If you just ask for a series of names, dates and places, you'll wear out your welcome in a hurry. Could you answer a series of rapid-fire questions about all the events in your life? It's better to ask leading, open-ended questions and gently guide the conversation toward your research objective.

People's memories operate in a strange way. There's a gap sometimes, especially for older folks, between the time the question is asked and when the answer pops up in their brains. That gap is often a week or ten days. You'll be amazed if you return after that interval and ask your questions again. Those memories and the answers to your questions may have surfaced.

Don't put off interviewing older relatives. They may not be around when you find time to visit and interview them. Go back. After you've talked with your relatives, go and do some research in census and courthouse records. Take your findings and revisit those relatives and ask for more details. A researcher had talked with relatives about her great-grandfather. They'd told her what a lovely person he'd been; such a kind and considerate old soul, they said. His newspaper obituary echoed those sentiments. But when she visited the courthouse, she found records showing her great-grandfather had paid several fines for "breach of the peace." When she asked the relatives for more information, they told her that the old boy had relived the Civil War on more than one occasion with a neighbor who'd fought on the other side.

If you want to read more about interview techniques, check at your local library for books on conducting oral history interviews. Also look at textbooks that help college students become news reporters. Specifically for genealogists, Gary L. Shumway and William G. Hartley have written *An Oral History Primer*.

Visiting Family Cemeteries

Older family members often make frequent trips to cemeteries where family members are buried. In rural areas, "cemetery working days" are popular. People with relatives buried in a particular country cemetery gather on an appointed day, often in the spring, and clean up the graveyard. They bring rakes and weed trimmers and a potluck lunch. It's an ideal time to meet distant cousins and gather genealogy information. Remember to take a rake to the event in addition to your notepad, so you'll blend in.

Depending upon the kind of cemetery where your relatives are buried, there may or may not be information available. In some very remote, rural cemeteries the stones may have fallen over and the cemetery may have virtually disappeared. No one in the area may remember who the graves belong to, and no records may exist about the burials.

Many families established burial grounds on their own family farms. They may be located far from roads. If the farm or land isn't still currently owned by the family, the burial ground may have fallen into neglect. Though most all states have laws that allow access to cemeteries, even those on private property, it isn't a good idea to visit those cemeteries without permission from the landowner in the area.

Visiting remote cemeteries can be dangerous. When your great-aunt reminded you it was bad luck to walk on someone's grave, she was right—it is downright dangerous because the ground may give way under your weight. Never go alone to remote areas. Plan your visit for a time of year that *isn't* hunting season. Genealogists know the best time of year to visit cemeteries that aren't well maintained is in the dead of winter when vegetation and crawling critters are at a low ebb, unless of course the cemetery is knee-deep in snow.

Cemetery names change. The newspaper obituary you found from eighty years ago may say an ancestor was buried in "Pickens Cemetery."

You search in vain for a cemetery by that name, only to have someone tell you it's known today as "Hawkins Cemetery" because the Hawkins family burials outnumber everyone else's. Or you find "Mt. Zion" cemetery mentioned on a death certificate, and don't find the gravestone for your ancestor in that cemetery. You learn later there is an "Old Mt. Zion" and a "New Mt. Zion." You, of course, searched the wrong cemetery.

Think about your ancestor's life when you begin a search for the burial place. If, for example, your ancestor was Jewish, he may not be buried in a local cemetery; he may have been buried in a nearby city in a Jewish cemetery. If your ancestor died away from home, her body may have been transported home for burial. Or your ailing ancestor who went to a health spa may have died in that place and the burial may have taken place nearby. The city of Hot Springs, Arkansas has people from all over the world buried in its cemeteries because the mineral baths were thought to be a cure for serious illnesses. People came there and died, and were buried in area cemeteries. If your ancestor was a veteran and died after the Civil War, he may have been buried in a national cemetery maintained by the federal government.

If the cemetery where your family members are buried is connected to a church, there may be records about the burials among the church's records. Through the mid-twentieth century, churches often had adjacent burial grounds. After World War II, however, large commercially run cemeteries began to replace family graveyards and church plots. Many cities maintain public cemeteries. If your family members are buried in large, well-maintained perpetual-care cemeteries, an employee may have detailed information not only about the burials, but also about who purchased the lots. City cemeteries usually have records about the burials.

Whatever kind of cemetery you find, pay attention to the people buried near your relatives—they may be family members, too. A researcher noticed an unfamiliar name on a gravemarker in the family plot. Further research showed the mystery marker belonged to the ancestor's mother-in-law, and opened a whole new family line.

Sifting Through Family Papers

Look through family papers for income tax returns, bank statements, insurance policies, voter registrations, military discharges, deeds and mortgages and any records that might give you addresses and places of residence, and possibly Social Security numbers for family members. You'll find some families kept an abundance of family papers, others kept little. Some families were prolific letter writers, others left no written records.

Whatever the number of family records available, go through them carefully. Make photocopies of all the papers that might potentially be of use to your search. And write on the copies the name of the person from whom you received the material.

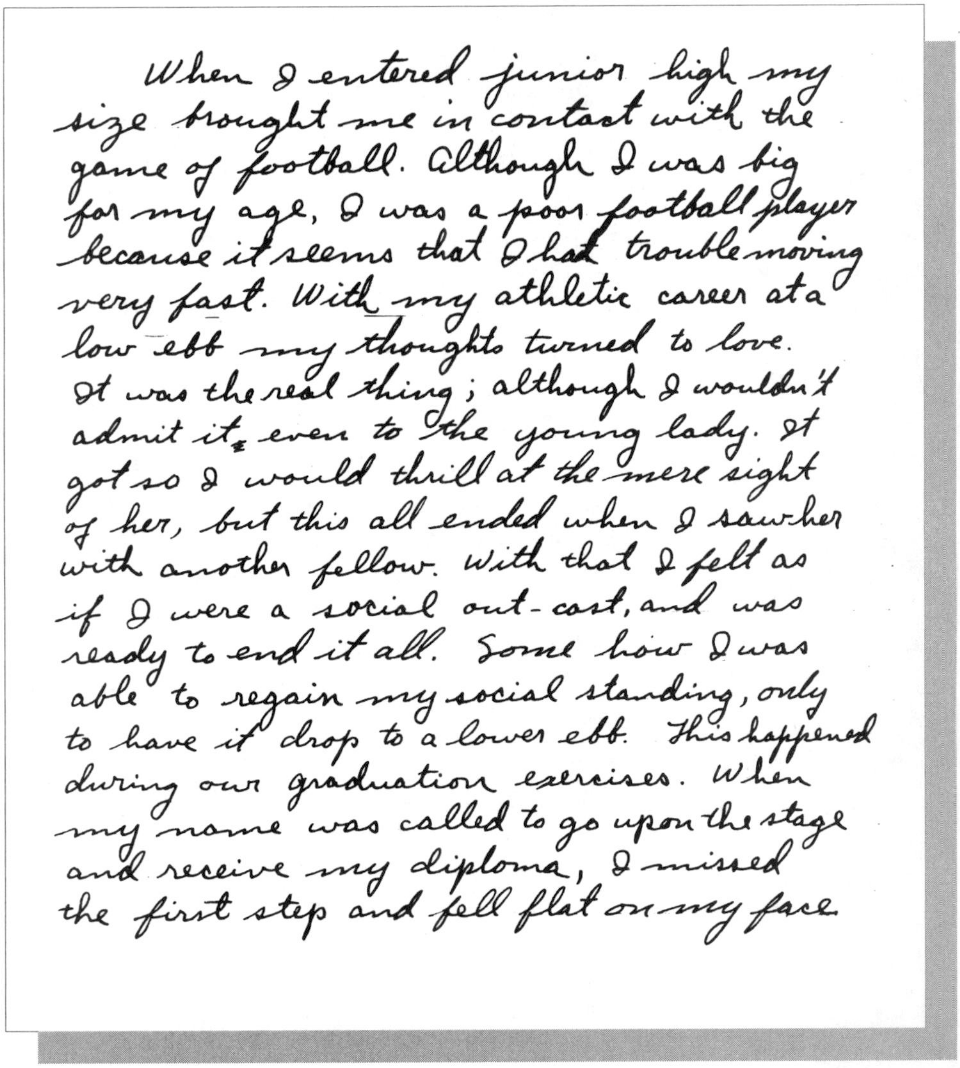

When I entered junior high my size brought me in contact with the game of football. Although I was big for my age, I was a poor football player because it seems that I had trouble moving very fast. With my athletic career at a low ebb my thoughts turned to love. It was the real thing; although I wouldn't admit it, even to the young lady. It got so I would thrill at the mere sight of her, but this all ended when I saw her with another fellow. With that I felt as if I were a social out-cast, and was ready to end it all. Some how I was able to regain my social standing, only to have it drop to a lower ebb. This happened during our graduation exercises. When my name was called to go upon the stage and receive my diploma, I missed the first step and fell flat on my face.

Figure 4-1: Enlightenment by Journal While cleaning the garage in preparation for a move, one genealogist found her father's journal tucked into one of his old college textbooks. The journal was apparently an assignment for a class and had lain in a trunk undisturbed since the 1930s. As you can see from the entry reproduced here, documents like this can lend remarkable insight into the lives and personalities of our ancestors.

Try to build a chronology of all the places you've lived since your birth. Then do the same for your parents. Remember to note your sources for the facts you find.

If you find family papers in the possession of your parents and grandparents with names on them you don't recognize, be aware the names may have significance later as your research progresses. Look, too, at the spelling of names in the documents. Your family names may have been spelled differently by various clerks who created the documents you uncover.

When you begin your search in family papers, look for copies of vital record certificates—such as birth and death certificates. A death certificate should contain the name of the cemetery where the deceased person was buried. A death certificate for one of your aunts or uncles may lead you to a family cemetery where your great-grandparents, who died before deaths were recorded on a statewide basis, are buried.

Frequently, family cemeteries are far removed from your present residence. You may not be able to go to the family cemetery, but someone may have compiled a published inventory. We'll talk more about finding that sort of resource in "Step 6, Branching Out: Beginning Research in Libraries and Archives," page 53.

Studying Family Photographs

Study family photos. Identifying information written on the backs may offer clues to relationships. "Your aunt, Bertha Barham," was written on the back of a photo in a researcher's collection. She didn't know who Bertha was, or whose aunt she'd been, but since the photo was among those preserved by the family, she knew Bertha must be a relative. Eventually, she discovered her great-grandmother had a sister Bertha. Further research turned up a marriage of that Bertha to a Mr. Barham. When Bertha's descendants were located, they were delighted to receive a copy of the photo. And they were able to share Bertha's parents' family Bible with the researcher.

Look for photographers' logos on photos that might tell you a place name. One photograph of two young boys had nothing written on the back about their identities, but the photographer's mark on the border of the photo said, "Purcell, I.T." I.T. was a commonly used abbreviation for "Indian Territory," an area that became eastern Oklahoma after statehood in 1907. A check of records in that place revealed information about a lost branch of the family. Previously unknown family members there recognized the boys in the photo. Their branch of the family had preserved letters received in the late nineteenth century from the researcher's family members.

Locating Vital Records

A favorite place to record family vital information in previous years was the family Bible. If you're lucky enough to locate one for your family, attempt to photocopy the family record pages and the title page of the Bible. If the Bible is very old or fragile, you may have to transcribe the information from it, but a photocopy is preferable. Check for loose papers inserted in the Bible—you may find newspaper obituary clippings or funeral memorial cards. But don't remove them from their original place—they may mark favorite or meaningful Bible passages. Be sure to make notes about who has the Bible now and who the former owners of the Bible were. You may find some family members very possessive about their ownership of a family Bible. Assure them you just want the *information*, and offer to share future research results with them.

After you've talked with relatives, searched through the family papers you can locate and visited family cemeteries, it's time to order copies of vital records. An inexpensive booklet, *Where to Write for Vital Records*, is available from the Government Printing Office. The booklet lists the addresses of state vital records offices and includes information about the dates when the various states began keeping birth and death records on a statewide basis. (See "Vital Records" in the Resources section, Appendix B, for details on where to obtain the booklet.) If, for example, your grandmother died in Arkansas in 1911, there's no need to order a search of the death records, because Arkansas didn't begin keeping statewide records until February, 1914. But if that same grandmother died in Missouri, there might be a certificate on file for her, as Missouri's consistent, statewide records begin in 1910.

Operators on Social Security Administration's toll-free telephone information line can also provide information about where to write to request birth and death records. Be sure to ask about *when* vital registration began for the state you're interested in, as well as where to write for the record. You can also learn the addresses of state vital records offices by asking the reference librarian at your local library. In addition, there are Internet sources for vital record agency addresses. (See the Resources section.)

After you've learned whether statewide vital records were kept in the particular state you're interested in for the time period when your ancestors were born or died, request copies of the certificates from the appropriate office. Some vital records offices require that you use their particular form to submit requests; others accept letters containing the search elements they need to find the correct record. In nearly all cases, the fee you send with your request is a *search* fee; if they don't find the record, they keep your money. So make every effort to send complete, correct details when you order.

Just because there *should* be a state vital record doesn't mean there will be. Compliance with the laws requiring registration of births and deaths wasn't universal in the early years. The event may never have been reported. Or the record may have been lost. Or the record may be there, but the name is misspelled either on the original or in the index and it can't be located. Vital records can potentially be very rewarding, however, so it's worth the effort.

Armed with the vital records you've ordered and all the other family information you've gathered, it's time to organize your materials before you delve into research in libraries and archives.

Privacy Laws

When you begin your genealogical research, begin with yourself. Public records about *you* are available to *you* because you have a right to that information. When you begin making inquiries about other people, even though they're related to you, you must consider privacy laws.

You wouldn't want personal information about yourself available to just anyone, would you? Much of it is already public record. In most counties, marriage and divorce records are open to any researcher, but those same records at the state level may be restricted by privacy laws. Some states restrict access, even at the county level, to records less than fifty years old. The custodian of the records you're interested in will be familiar with the restrictions on the records in that jurisdiction.

Do you remember when the federal census was last taken? You were required by law to fill out the forms or otherwise answer the questions, but you were assured the information would be kept private. And it is kept private for seventy-two years. You can obtain copies of information from unreleased census records about *yourself* from the Personal Service Branch, Bureau of the Census, P.O. Box 1545, Jeffersonville, Indiana 47131. Write and ask for Form BC-600 to learn about the fees and requirements. Some people who do not have birth certificates on file use this unreleased census information as proof of age to support an application for a delayed birth certificate.

The Social Security Administration will furnish information about *deceased* people to anyone, regardless of relationship. Deceased people have no privacy rights, according to federal policies. But you have to prove the person you're inquiring about is dead.

Military service records for people who served in the armed forces in the last seventy-five years are protected by privacy laws. Most of these records are housed at the National Personnel Records Center, 9700 Page Boulevard, St. Louis, Missouri 63132. However, under the 1974 Freedom of Information Law, some data from the records can be released to people other than the serviceperson.

Release of information in private records is up to the record holder. Funeral homes, for example, are private, commercial concerns. They usually furnish information to genealogists about people for whom they've conducted services, but they're under no obligation to do so. Hospitals are very careful about releasing any information that would violate a person's privacy.

Most privacy laws allow you to request information about a living person if that person signs a release. You've encountered this when your insurance company asks you to sign a release so medical information about you from a doctor or hospital can be sent to the company.

It's frustrating to have your research reach a stopping point because of privacy laws, but remember that *your* privacy is protected as well.

After you've gathered all the records about your family that are available to you, it's time to organize the material and assess your information so you'll know where to begin your search in libraries and archives.

STEP 5

A PLACE FOR EVERYTHING
Keeping Records

If you don't start organizing your genealogical materials as you collect them, you're going to get very confused somewhere down the road. If you've already started collecting materials, it's time to put them into some kind of order before you get discouraged about the amount of time it takes you to find a particular piece of information in your records.

On the other hand, you can get so bogged down in organizing papers that you lose sight of your objective and don't have time to do actual research. So strike a balance between chaos and obsessive neatness. Think about the person who might find your genealogy research notes when you're no longer available—will your organizational system be self-evident? Can that person pick up your work and continue? Even more important, if you lay your genealogy aside for a few years, can you come back to it and retrieve your train of thought?

You can devise a perfectly manageable system with note paper and file folders, which is described below. If you want a more structured approach, try William Dollarhide's *Managing a Genealogical Project*. It's a paper system that offers a sensible approach with plenty of forms and a numbering system.

Computers make wonderful organizational tools and there are dozens of fine software programs on the market for managing a genealogical database. Choose a program that will let you enter a source note with each event in an ancestor's life. (Some only offer one "notes" field per person.) Programs today let you attach scanned photographs and audio and video clips to data. When you reach the stage of writing about your family's history, computer programs will greatly simplify your task.

Computer programs don't do your research for you. It's up to you to find information about your ancestors and enter it into the program you've chosen, along with source information. The software will help you organize and display your information, but *you* must do the evaluation and analysis of what you've found.

Creating Family Group Sheets

Start your organizational system around nuclear families—one set of parents and their children. Begin with yourself. If you're a married person, make a family group sheet for yourself and your spouse and your children, if you have any. A family group sheet can be a preprinted form, or simply a sheet of paper with a summary about one family written in a consistent manner. The group sheets reproduced in figures 5-1 and 5-2 are only two examples of how to organize your information; recording *all* your information *consistently* is more important than using any one form.

Preprinted forms are available from a number of genealogical vendors. Their addresses are listed in the Resources section (Appendix B) of this book. Genealogy computer programs take the information you enter and organize family group sheets for you to print out.

You can make your own family group sheets with notebook paper. For each nuclear family, record the following information:

About the husband, list

- his name
- his birth date and birth place
- marriage date and place (to the wife listed on *this* sheet)
- death date and place, and place of burial
- places of residence, occupation and religious affiliation
- military service
- other wives (make separate group sheets for each marriage, just note the names of other wives on this sheet)
- father's name
- mother's maiden name

About the wife, list:

- her name
- her birth date and birth place
- death date and place, and place of burial
- places of residence, occupation and religious affiliation
- military service
- other husbands (make separate group sheets for each marriage; just note the names of other husbands on this sheet)
- father's name
- mother's maiden name

List the children born to *this* husband and wife (arrange them in birth order):

- sex
- name
- birth date and birth place
- marriage date and place
- spouse's name
- death date and place, and place of burial

About the compiler, list:
- your complete name and address
- the date you filled out this family group sheet

As you write in facts about the people on the sheet or form, make very specific notes about where you learned each piece of information. Put those notes on the back of the group sheet, using the source guide in the back of this book to tell you what data elements to record about each source. Number your source list. Use those numbers you've assigned to your sources to indicate exactly what pieces of information on your group sheet came from each source.

For example, if you use your birth certificate as the source of information about your date and place of birth and your parents' names, then your source notation might read something like this, "State of Ohio Birth Certificate #9-87654-321 for Terry Smith." If you've listed that item as source number two on your family group sheet, then place a "2" beside each data item supported by the birth certificate. If information is supplied verbally by a relative, write the person's name, address and the date you heard the information. If you're writing in your marriage date or the births of your children, you might list yourself as the source, because you were present for the events. Of course, you were present at your birth, too, but you weren't a very reliable witness at the time.

Be consistent about the way you write dates (see the discussion in "Step 2, Playing Sherlock Holmes: The Genealogist's Skills and Goals," pages 7-8). Most genealogists write dates with the day of the month first, then the month spelled out as a word, followed by the year as a four-digit number. Thus, 25 July 1950. Also be consistent about the way you write place names. Write the city, town or village name first, then the county, followed by the state, for places within the United States. For foreign countries, use the same format—local name, province, country.

After you've filled out a family group sheet for your family, complete one with your parents as the couple at the top of the sheet, and list yourself as one of the children on the form. Then complete group sheets for your mother's parents and your father's parents.

You may find one group sheet doesn't supply enough room for all your sources or all the children of a particular couple. Simply write "continued on page 2" in the bottom margin and note "continued from previous page," on the top of the second sheet. You need not repeat all the details about the couple, just re-enter their names at the top of the second page.

You should fill out group sheets for *each marriage*. If you're using a computer program, it will automatically generate a group sheet for each married couple. Some people will be listed on more than one group sheet. If your grandmother was married three times and had children by all three of her husbands, there should be three separate sheets for her, one with each husband, listing just the children from that union. Note cross-references on each sheet to help you remember there were other marriages. Don't just make a group sheet for the couple from whom you're descended—you'll omit some of your cousins from your family history. Remember—one group sheet per marriage.

Put your name and address on each group sheet. If you leave one you're working on at the library, it can find its way home. If you share one with other genealogists, they'll know who created it.

Constructing Pedigree Charts

You can mentally organize your ancestors for the first two or three recent generations. After that, your family tree can resemble a thicket instead of a single tree if you don't create a pedigree chart to help you visualize your direct lineage. Unlike group sheets, pedigree charts only show your direct ancestors. Grandfather's brothers and sisters are included on a family group sheet for your great-grandparents, but only your grandparents and their parents (and their parents and so on) are listed on a pedigree chart.

If you're using a computer program, you can automatically generate a pedigree chart from the data you've entered. With a paper system, you'll have to fill out a pedigree chart using the information on your group sheets. You'll use the pedigree chart to share your *lineage* information with other researchers. Pedigree charts are available in a variety of styles and sizes from the genealogical vendors listed in the Resources section of this book, and a sample chart is reproduced in Figure 5-3.

People on your pedigree chart are numbered in a particular way. You're number 1. (You *knew* that!) Your father is number 2 on the chart; your mother is number 3. Your father's father is number 4; your father's mother is number 5; your mother's father is number 6; and her mother's mother is number 7. You'll notice a pattern developing here. Except for number 1 (that's you), all the men on the chart have even numbers, and all the women have odd numbers. Any person on the chart's father's number is twice their number. Thus, your mother's father's number is 6, twice that of your mother's number which is 3. Your mother's father's father's number is 12. A wife's number is always one more than her husband's number. Your father's lines are called your "paternal" lines and occupy the top half of your pedigree chart; you mother's are your "maternal" lines, and occupy the bottom half.

Family Group Sheet

Husband's Full Name

Date of:	Day Month Year	Town	County	State or Country	Additional Info.
Birth:					
Marriage:					
Death:					
Burial:					
Places of Residence:					
Occupation:		Religion:		Military Record:	
Other wives:					
His father:			His mother:		

Information Obtained From:

Wife's Full Maiden Name

Date of:	Day Month Year	Town	County	State or Country	Additional Info.
Birth:					
Marriage:					
Death:					
Burial:					
Places of Residence:					
Occupation, if other than Housewife:				Religion:	
Other husbands:					
Her father:			Her mother:		

Compiler:

Address:

City:

State:

Date:

Sex:	Children's Full Names:	Date of:	Day Month Year	Town	County	State or Country	Additional Info.
	1.	Birth:					
		Marriage:					
	Full Name of Spouse:	Death:					
		Burial:					
	2.	Birth:					
		Marriage:					
	Full Name of Spouse:	Death:					
		Burial:					
	3.	Birth:					
		Marriage:					
	Full Name of Spouse:	Death:					
		Burial:					
	4.	Birth:					
		Marriage:					
	Full Name of Spouse:	Death:					
		Burial:					
	5.	Birth:					
		Marriage:					
	Full Name of Spouse:	Death:					
		Burial:					
	6.	Birth:					
		Marriage:					
	Full Name of Spouse:	Death:					
		Burial:					
	7.	Birth:					
		Marriage:					
	Full Name of Spouse:	Death:					
		Burial:					
	8.	Birth:					
		Marriage:					
	Full Name of Spouse:	Death:					
		Burial:					

Figure 5-1: Family Group Sheet

Additional Children

Sex:	Children's Full Names:	Date of:	Day Month Year	Town	Count_	State or Country	Additional Info.
	9.	Birth:					
		Marriage:					
	Full Name of Spouse:	Death:					
		Burial:					
	10.	Birth:					
		Marriage:					
	Full Name of Spouse:	Death:					
		Burial:					
	11.	Birth:					
		Marriage:					
	Full Name of Spouse:	Death:					
		Burial:					
	12.	Birth:					
		Marriage:					
	Full Name of Spouse:	Death:					
		Burial:					
	13.	Birth:					
		Marriage:					
	Full Name of Spouse:	Death:					
		Burial:					
	14.	Birth:					
		Marriage:					
	Full Name of Spouse:	Death:					
		Burial:					
	15.	Birth:					
		Marriage:					
	Full Name of Spouse:	Death:					
		Burial:					
	16.	Birth:					
		Marriage:					
	Full Name of Spouse:	Death:					
		Burial:					

Additional Sources

FAMILY GROUP SHEET

Use boxes below to record source number codes from the list on the back of this form.

FATHER'S NAME _____ ☐

Date of birth _____ ☐ Place _____ ☐

Date of death_____ ☐ Place _____ ☐

Date of burial_____ ☐ Cemetery & Place _____ ☐

Date of marriage_____ ☐ Place _____ ☐

Father _____ ☐ Mother & Maiden Name _____ ☐

Other Wives_____ ☐

Date of Divorce_____ ☐ Place of Divorce _____ ☐

MOTHER'S MAIDEN NAME_____ ☐

Date of birth _____ ☐ Place _____ ☐

Date of death_____ ☐ Place _____ ☐

Date of burial_____ ☐ Cemetery & Place _____ ☐

Father _____ ☐ Mother & Maiden Name _____ ☐

Other Husbands _____ ☐

Date of Divorce_____ ☐ Place of Divorce _____ ☐

Sex	Children In order of birth	Src	Birth	Src	Death	Src	Marriage	Src
1	Name		Date		Date		Date	
	Spouse		Place		Place		Place	
2	Name		Date		Date		Date	
	Spouse		Place		Place		Place	
3	Name		Date		Date		Date	
	Spouse		Place		Place		Place	
4	Name		Date		Date		Date	
	Spouse		Place		Place		Place	
5	Name		Date		Date		Date	
	Spouse		Place		Place		Place	
6	Name		Date		Date		Date	
	Spouse		Place		Place		Place	
7	Name		Date		Date		Date	
	Spouse		Place		Place		Place	
8	Name		Date		Date		Date	
	Spouse		Place		Place		Place	
9	Name		Date		Date		Date	
	Spouse		Place		Place		Place	

DGS

©1996 Dallas Genealogical Society, P.O. Box 12648, Dallas, Texas 75225
Form 2fh.96

Figure 5-2: Family Group Sheet

S e x	Children In order of birth	S r c	Birth	S r c	Death	S r c	Marriage	S r c
10	Name		Date		Date		Date	
	Spouse		Place		Place		Place	
11	Name		Date		Date		Date	
	Spouse		Place		Place		Place	
12	Name		Date		Date		Date	
	Spouse		Place		Place		Place	
13	Name		Date		Date		Date	
	Spouse		Place		Place		Place	
14	Name		Date		Date		Date	
	Spouse		Place		Place		Place	

NOTES: Items of interest about this family such as occupations, military service, dates of immigration, physical description, residences, achievements, higher education, religious, social, civil, political, cause of death, moves, present address, etc.

SOURCE CITATIONS: Place exact reference after type of source.
Example: Deed—Dallas Co, TX, Deed Bk A, p. 6
Bible—Aunt Mary Wilson's, King James version in possession of son Terry Wilson, Waco, TX.

1. Bible _____
2. Census _____
   _____
   _____
3. Church _____
4. Correspondence _____
   _____
   _____
5. Court _____
6. Deed _____
7. Published History _____
8. Interviews/Oral History _____
9. Military _____
10. Obituary _____

11. Tombstone _____
12. Vital Records:
    Birth Certificate _____
    Marriage Certificate _____
    Death Certificate _____
13. Newspaper _____
14. Will/Estate Settlement/Guardianship _____
    _____
15. Funeral Home _____
16. Photos _____
    _____
17. Personal Knowledge * _____
18. Other _____
    _____

* Source should be corroborated with written records.

Form of Source:
a. Original   b. Certified Copy   c. Recorded copy   d. Transcribed copy   e. Extract
f. Photo copy   g. Handwritten   h. Typewritten   i. Printed

Compiler:_____ Telephone:_____

Address_____ City_____ State_____ Zip_____

Pedigree Chart

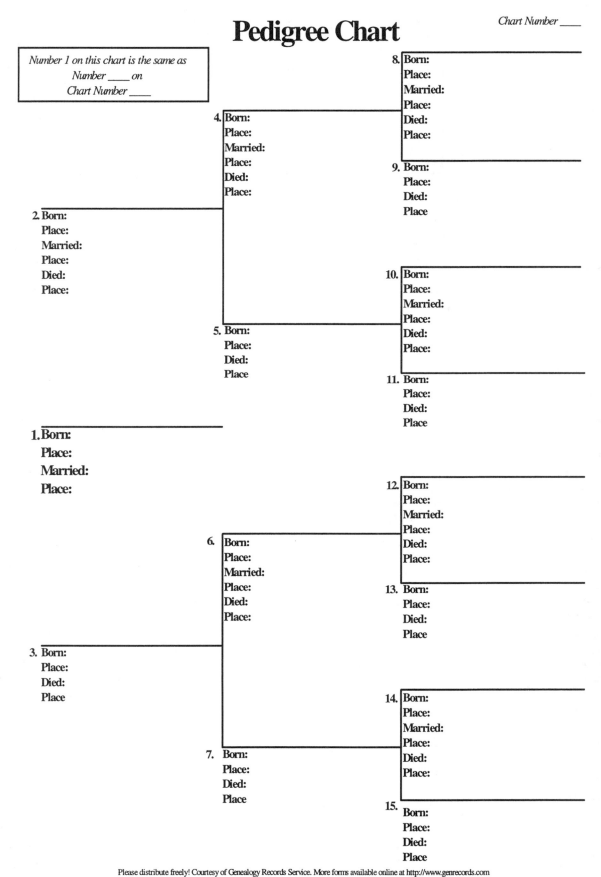

Number 1 on this chart is the same as Number ____ on Chart Number ____

8. Born:
Place:
Married:
Place:
Died:
Place:

4. Born:
Place:
Married:
Place:
Died:
Place:

9. Born:
Place:
Died:
Place

2. Born:
Place:
Married:
Place:
Died:
Place:

10. Born:
Place:
Married:
Place:
Died:
Place:

5. Born:
Place:
Died:
Place

11. Born:
Place:
Died:
Place

1. Born:
Place:
Married:
Place:

12. Born:
Place:
Married:
Place:
Died:
Place:

6. Born:
Place:
Married:
Place:
Died:
Place:

13. Born:
Place:
Died:
Place

3. Born:
Place:
Died:
Place

14. Born:
Place:
Married:
Place:
Died:
Place:

7. Born:
Place:
Died:
Place

15. Born:
Place:
Died:
Place

Figure 5-3: Pedigree Chart

One kind of printout you can request from most genealogy computer programs is an "ancestor chart," also sometimes called an "*ahnentafel* chart." These charts use the same numbering system found on pedigree charts.

Filling out family group sheets and pedigree charts can help you mentally organize your information. They're graphic representations of the data you've collected. Remember when you were in school and you listened to instructors' lectures? You probably remembered more if you took notes. But if you took the information and had to make a diagram or chart from it, then you probably really learned it. It's the same with group sheets and pedigree charts, even though there's not going to be a quiz over who your ancestors were.

Note Taking

You'll find yourself taking notes as you study materials about your family. Your note taking may start with some jotted remarks made during a conversation with a family member. As soon as you find yourself writing information about your family, start making an effort at consistent, systematic note keeping.

Don't grab any scratch pad at hand. And don't reach for a spiral notebook, the kind that leaves ragged edges on the pages when you tear a sheet out. You remember that kind of notebook—your teacher told you she'd count points off if you turned in an assignment with those ragged edges. If you're a bit older than the spiral notebook generation, you remember the Big Chief tablets. The paper in them was lined newsprint, and if you kept some of that paper around for a few years, it turned yellow and brittle. Don't use that kind, either. The acid used in the papermaking process is what caused that paper to age.

Nearly all kinds of paper used to be manufactured with an acid process. Even books were produced on acid-filled paper. Then librarians took a hard look at what was happening to old books. They were crumbling. The books printed before the Civil War seemed to be aging well, but those manufactured from the time of the War onward were deteriorating badly. The culprit was acid used to break down the wood fibers to make the paper. Before the War, paper was made with a different process. Rag fibers were used instead of cellulose or wood pulp. Paper was expensive, but durable. When the process changed, paper became much cheaper, but it was filled with acid, a built-in time bomb.

It was possible, but expensive, to make acid-free paper. Book manufacturers began to demand it. The Library of Congress established standards for permanence. Genealogists began to use acid-free paper for their notes and charts, even though a ream of acid-free paper used to cost several times the price of ordinary paper. A couple of decades ago, some people who were worried about our environment became concerned about where the acid was going after it was used in the papermaking plants. Costly prohibitions were put in place to clean up the problem. Paper companies have begun switching to newer, better papermaking processes that don't use acid. As a result, you can buy inexpensive alkaline-based paper that won't deteriorate like the paper manufactured with acid.

To learn whether a paper is acid- or alkaline-based, call the paper manufacturer whose label is on the ream of paper. Most have toll-free numbers you can obtain by calling (800) 555-1212 or by checking the toll-free directory on the Internet. For a way to test paper for its acid content, see the sidebar in this chapter, "But How Do I Know If It's Acid-Free?"

Use standard-sized, nonacid-based (alkaline) paper for your notes. Don't use the backs of envelopes or "scratch" paper. Stick with good quality 8½″×11″ paper. If you're printing information from your computer program, use alkaline paper in your printer.

Avoid using metal clips and rubber bands in the materials you're going to keep in your files for a long time. *Never* use transparent tape of any kind. Metal clips will eventually rust and make ugly stains on the paper they touch. Use plastic or plastic-coated wire paper clips instead. Rubber bands turn into nasty things as they age. They're just innocent-looking rubber bands when you use them, but hidden in your files, they take on a new life and become sticky, gummy monsters. Swear off rubber bands. Transparent tape of any kind should never find a home in your papers. Like rubber bands, it looks helpful, then becomes a nightmare in a few years. It turns yellow and adhesive oozes out from its edges and damages and stains everything within reach. Eventually (after the damage) it dies and turns loose the paper it was applied to.

Think about where you're going to file your notes and only record information about one family on a sheet of paper. Note your source first. At the top of the page, write the name of the family the notes pertain to. If the notes need to be filed in more than one folder, you can either photocopy them to make a second copy, or place a cross-reference note in the second folder.

Don't recopy your notes. Every time you transcribe or copy anything, you're introducing a possible new set of errors. You're also wasting time. Make your notes neat enough the first time to use without recopying. Verify what you've written. It only takes a few minutes to look back over what you've written and compare it with your source to ensure you didn't miscopy or leave out any important element.

You may need to photocopy your notes, so use black ink or a soft-lead pencil. Blue ink or a hard-lead pencil may not show up when reproduced on a photocopier. Some libraries and archives only permit the use of pencils in their facility, so take along your own that produce a black-enough mark to be photocopied.

A laptop computer can be very helpful in taking notes in a library, especially if you're used to typing instead of writing. Be sure computers are permitted before you start to use one. Some archives require that you leave

But How Do I Know If It's Acid-Free?

Paper manufactured with an acid process will eventually discolor and become brittle. After that, it begins to crumble. Newsprint is the worst offender; you can watch it deteriorate in a matter of weeks. But newsprint isn't made to be permanent—we throw away yesterday's newspaper. Pick up a paperback novel printed twenty years ago. The pages are brown, and if you turn down the corner of a page, it'll break off. But paperback novels weren't meant to be permanent, either. Now think about your genealogy materials. They *are* meant to be permanent.

But if you use paper manufactured with an acid process for your genealogy notes and forms, they won't be around for your descendants to read. To combat this problem, use acid-free or alkaline-based paper. You may think buying a good grade of cotton-content paper will ensure freedom from acid. It's not so. Even expensive paper may have an acid content, and it will deteriorate.

How can you tell if paper is safe? If the paper you're curious about is packaged in a ream from a paper manufacturer, read the label—it may tell you whether it's an alkaline-based paper. If it doesn't, you can call the paper manufacturer and ask. Most companies have toll-free numbers. Many paper companies have posted informational Web sites on the Internet offering information about their products.

But what if the paper you want to use for your genealogy notes or in your computer printer isn't labeled with a manufacturer's brand name? How are you going to find out if the paper is acid-free? Use the same method librarians use; test the paper with an Abbey pH Pen.

An Abbey pH Pen looks like a Sharpie marker, but it isn't a writing instrument. It's filled with a chemical called chlorophenol red. You just uncap the pen and mark on the paper in question. If the mark is purple, no acid is present; if the mark is yellow, the paper contains acid.

Chlorophenol red is a pH indicator, a kind of chemical that changes color at certain levels of acidity or alkalinity. William J. Barrow, the pioneer of document deacidification and permanent paper from the 1940s to 1967, tested many naturally aged book papers using a chlorophenol red solution. He reported a visible color change for the chemical occurring between 6.0 and 6.7 on the pH scale. Chlorophenol red reliably changes color at the same pH regardless of the concentration of the solution. That property makes it a reliable, accurate way to test for acid in paper.

The Abbey pH Pen is available from Abbey Publications, Inc., 7105 Geneva Drive, Austin, Texas 78723, and also from library supply houses, such as Gaylord Brothers, Inc., P.O. Box 4901, Syracuse, New York 13221.

your coat, briefcase, and any other personal objects in a locker before using original manuscript materials. You may be permitted to take in only a single pencil and two sheets of notebook paper. Think positive: at least you're allowed to keep your clothes on, and the next time you want to use the materials, they'll be there.

Sometimes, the time you have to spend in a library is limited. When possible, photocopy the materials you need to take information from. Be sure to photocopy the title page of a book or periodical and check to be sure it has all the elements you'll need to write a complete source citation. Note the repository, too. Genealogy books are often printed in very small press runs and you may wonder later where you found a particular book if you have to refer to it again. If you plan to reuse the book in that same library, note the call number in your notes. The call number may be different in another library, but make a note of it, since it will save time in retrieving the book the next time you need to use it in that library.

A Research Calendar

A list of the sources you've searched is called by various names: research calendar, research log, source organizer, research index or something else. Whatever you call it, a research calendar helps you keep track of the materials you've searched. It's essentially a list of sources you've examined. Figure 5-4 shows a blank research calendar, and figure 5-5 shows the same calendar filled out.

You may need a research calendar for each surname you're working on. Or you may want to make one for each locality you're researching. Try the locality method first, and if it doesn't work out, change your method of keeping up with the sources you've searched to suit your research habits.

If, for example, you're working on Randolph County, North Carolina, you may have more than one family line that lived in that place. If you made research calendars for each surname, you'd have to write your entries on more than one calendar.

To create a research calendar, label a sheet of paper with the title you've assigned to it: "Randolph County, North Carolina, Research Calendar," for example. Be sure to put your name, address and phone number on the page in the event you accidentally abandon it after a hard day at the library. Make ruled columns on the page and label them "Source," "Purpose," "Notes," "Date" and "Repository."

When you visit the library (which we'll do in "Step 6, Branching Out: Beginning Research in Libraries and Archives," page 53) and find a book that might contain information on your family, pull out your research calendar and make an entry for that source. List author, title, date and place of publication, and publisher. In the "Purpose" column, write the surnames you're looking for. Note the date and repository, too. You might want to develop abbreviations for the repositories you frequently use: ACPL for Allen County, Indiana, Public Library, or CL for Houston's Clayton Library.

If you didn't find anything of interest in the book, write "nothing located" or something like that in the "Notes" column in your research calendar. Why list a book that didn't help you? Someday you might see that book's title in a bibliography or some other source and you might spend

RESEARCH CALENDAR

Researcher:	Ancestor:
Locality: State / County / Town	Time period:

Brief problem statement:

Search Date	Where Available	Call #	Title / Author / Publisher / Year or Record Identification Information	Notes	Page #'s

Figure 5-4: Blank Research Calendar

Page __1__

RESEARCH CALENDAR

Researcher:	Bess Calhoun	Ancestor:	Ewing Murray
Locality: State / County / Town	Atchison, MO + Cherokee, KS	Time period:	1860+

Brief problem statement:

Identify children of Ewing Murray + Sarah Robertson

Search Date	Where Available	Call #	Title / Author / Publisher / Year or Record Identification Information	Notes	Page #'s
12 May 1997	Courthouse Atchison, MO	—	Intestate probate packet of James Robertson 17 Nov 1879	Names "sister Sarah Murry of Cherokee Co., KS"	—
"	"	—	Atchison Co. Marriage Book A 1845-1863	No marriage for Ewing + Sarah	—
29 May 1997	Dallas Public Library		1860 Census of Atchison Co, MO	Children: Mary E. 5, Jonathan 3, Emalisa 11/12	p. 525
"	"		1870 Census of Atchison Co, MO	Not there	
"	"		1870 Census of Cherokee Co, KS	Mary, Jonathan, Emalissa, George, Ella J., Samuel R, baby not named	p. 64
14 Jul 1997	"		1880 Census of Cherokee Co, KS	Johnathan, George, Ella, Samuel, Richard, E.Nves, Bessie	ED 41 p. 9
"	"	929.37819 S193C	The Marriages of Cherokee Co., KS 1867-1912. W. David Samuelson 1989 AIS/SLC	Records for Mary, Emalisa, George, Ella, Richard, Bessie	Copy all!
"	"	929.37819 Z19R	Affidavits of Death. Jeanne Zahn 1982 Cherokee Co.Gen.Soc.	No Ewing/Got Sarah Names heirs	Bk.A p.183
26 Jul 1997	"	T623 r474	1900 Census Cherokee Co, KS	Ewing + Sarah live w/ daughter Bessie	ED 38 p 5
"	"	929.37819 5355B	Baxter Springs Cemetery + Others. Marilyn Schmitt Cherokee Co.Gen.Soc 1983	Pence Cem.	Copy all
Oct 1997	Cherokee Co. GenWeb	—	History of Cherokee Co., KS + Representative Citizens. N.T. Allison 1904 Biographical Pub. Co. Chicago	Article on son-in-law Walther von Wedell	p. 549

Figure 5-5: Research Calendar Notice that this researcher not only wrote down what she found, but also what she *didn't* find. In the 1870 Census of Atchison County, Missouri, for instance, she found no listings for Ewing Murray or Sarah Robertson. By making a note of this, she will prevent herself from looking twice in the same place.

considerable time and effort locating that volume, just to be disappointed all over again. If you make a note about your negative search on the first encounter, it may save you some time later. Then again, you might discover another family line in that same location. You can pull out your research calendar and see that you did search that title but only for the Smith and Jones names, not the Abernathys. And you'd know you need to search it again for the new surname.

If you do find something of interest in the source you've searched, you can write the page numbers of the relevant pages on your calendar. Or you might write, "see notes." If the book isn't indexed and you only had time to scan the first three chapters, make a note of that, so you'll know where to pick up next time.

At first, when you check books that look promising, you'll only look for the names you recognize as your family lines. After a while, you'll wise up and begin to check for all the names of associates of your family. Your research calendar will help you remember what sources you need to go back to.

Some people use their research calendars as a sort of master source list. They write an abbreviation for a particular source on their research notes. You may *not* want to follow that plan. There's no guarantee your research calendar will always be available to go with your notes. It's probably a better idea to note complete source information on each of your research notes pages, in addition to writing the citation in your research calendar.

When you move from published sources to original records, a research calendar is especially valuable. If you read the entire census on microfilm for Randolph County, North Carolina, you would note that on your calendar. If, on the other hand, you just looked at the printed index, you'd make that distinction in your research calendar. And if you used a transcription instead of the census film itself, you'd note that, too, along with the name of the person who made the transcription and other publication information.

Keeping a research calendar takes discipline. If you develop the habit at the beginning of your genealogical research career, it will seem second-nature later on. And as you progress from a beginner to an advanced researcher, you'll earn respect from your peers who will appreciate your professional approach.

Filing Documents

As you begin this process of filling out family group sheets, you'll see the need to organize the documents from which you took information. Start a filing system based on your group sheets; that is, label a file folder for each family for whom you've made a group sheet. File folders made of acid-free paper are available from vendors of preservation materials. We've suggested some for you in the resource section. Acid-free folders cost more than garden-variety folders, but if you're planning to keep your records for a long time, they're a wise investment.

This may sound a bit sexist, but label the folder with the husband's name first, then the wife's. Only in recent times and on a limited basis have wives kept their birth (maiden) names as their surnames. Women did, and frequently still do, assume the surname of their husbands. So this is also the way most genealogical collections are organized. Then again, creativity in your research is a good thing, so if you feel strongly about this subject, put the woman's name first and arrange your filing system that way. Do be consistent, however, and label all your folders this way.

Put the documents you've found, or copies of the documents, in the folder for the family they concern. Your grandparents' marriage license, for example, will go in the folder you've labeled with their names. The information from that license, along with a note about your source, will go on their family group sheet.

If you're using a computer program, you might scan the important documents and store them on disk as graphic images. Some genealogy software programs will allow you to establish links between data items and image files. (If you haven't worked with a computer, this paragraph may sound like gibberish. It will all come together as you learn more about the advantages of computers in genealogical research.) Even if you scan the documents, you'll probably still want to store your originals in some order, and the easiest way is to organize them by family groups.

File the folders alphabetically according to the husband's name (there's that sexist problem again) if that's the way you've set up your folders. You can start out with a box sized to accommodate standard file folders. (These are available in acid-free materials, too.) Soon, you'll find yourself shopping for a file cabinet, then another. Genealogy is a paper-intensive business, even when you use a computer to organize your information.

File copies of your family group sheets in the folders with the families they're associated with. Photocopy the family group sheets for the families you're currently researching and put them in a three-ring notebook to take to the library. Leave all those source documents at home in their files. Remember, too, that anything you take with you when you leave home may be lost along the way. You don't want your only copies of your family group sheets to disappear when you leave your notebook in the library break room.

As a precaution, label your notebook and any other materials you routinely take with you to the library with your name, address and phone number. Consider putting "Reward for return" under your address if you're especially bad about leaving your possessions behind.

As you accumulate more and more research notes, you may periodically want to make security copies of your family group sheets and store them in a relative's home. If disaster strikes, your properly cited family group sheets would make it easier to recreate your research. If you're using a computer program and have Internet access, just attach the data file created by your genealogy program to an E-mail message and send it to someone who'll look after it. Compress it first with a program like PKZIP to speed up the process and take up less space on your friend's disk.

These family group sheets you've filled out or generated from computer information have another purpose. You'll find yourself writing to other researchers to ask for information. Don't be the person who says, "Send me everything you have on the Whatever family." (Substitute one of your family's surnames for "Whatever.") How will they know which materials you've already found? Instead, send a copy of your family group sheet on the family you have in common along with your pedigree chart so they can see how you're descended from their ancestor. If you've noted the sources you've used on the group sheet, your correspondent will have a list of the documents you've used, and will know which ones in their possession might be of most benefit to you.

You can file copies of your research calendar in your notebook with your group sheets for that particular family. Your research calendar needs to go with you to the library, but you might want to leave a photocopy of it at home.

Writing for Information

As you move from searching sources in your home, you'll begin to write letters and contact people who can help with additional information. Some contacts will be one-time events—just a letter and a response. Others will be ongoing. You may use electronic mail messages (E-mail) to replace traditional paper letters, but you'll probably be saving hard copies of those as well, the important ones at least.

You can file one-time correspondence, a request and reply about a marriage license for example, in the folder for the family it concerns. You might establish separate folders for the letters from your ongoing correspondents.

Communication is one of the mainstays of genealogical research. After you've talked with all the living relatives you can locate and surveyed the sources you can find at home, it's time to start writing for information.

Phone Communication

Yes, you can use the phone, but there are limits to phone conversations. People in the business world know the frustrations of playing "telephone tag," where you leave a message for someone and your call is returned, but you're away, so your answering machine takes the message, so you can make another attempt later. Your call may come at an inconvenient time for the person you're calling. You'll have no record of the information you learn in a call—unless you want to attempt to record the call, a tedious procedure, since you'd then have to transcribe the dialogue.

There are times to use the phone. Your call to the reference desk of the local library is probably appropriate if it conforms to library policy. Calling a newly found cousin to chat (after you've written and asked about a convenient time to call) can be fun. Calling your grandmother on a regular basis is a good idea, too.

Writing Letters

Letters can be mailed, sent through a facsimile machine (faxed), or sent through the phone lines through the Internet as electronic mail (E-mail) messages. Letters go to cousins, other researchers, repositories, courthouse offices, libraries, genealogy societies and others. Most all are your requests for information to help with your research. Some simple tips will make your correspondence more effective.

Be brief. More and more we're growing accustomed to receiving information in short bursts—sound bites. When we receive a letter, we want a quick idea of what the letter is about. So when you send one, don't offer meaningless detail. Do offer enough information to direct your request. Confine your request to one or two questions.

Be clear about what you're asking for. It's a good idea to have this notion worked out before you put fingers to keyboard or pen to paper.

Be nice. Remember your manners. Phrase your requests as just that—not demands. "Please" and "thank you" go a long way. Offer to pay for what you're requesting.

Direct your letter to the correct person or agency. Do a little preliminary research. If you're writing for a marriage record, be sure it's directed to the right clerk's office in the correct courthouse.

Confine your letter to one or two questions. Many repositories have a policy of only responding to one-question letters and directing a list of professional researchers to the writers of multiquestion letters. You can probably write again if you have more questions.

If you must handwrite your letters, be sure your handwriting is legible. Genealogists have enough trouble reading old records; don't add your letter to their handwriting woes.

When you're sending a traditional letter, add an "enclosure" note at the bottom, listing the documents you're including. Put the abbreviation, "Enc.:" at the left margin, below your signature, and list the items you're enclosing with your letter. It serves as a shopping list for you when you stuff the envelope, it lets your recipient know what to expect with the letter, and it's a handy reminder to review when you're writing the person again, so you won't send the same documents once more. Be sure to put your name and address on each of those enclosures in case they get separated from your letter.

Enclosures, called "attachments," can be made to E-mail messages as well, in the form of computer files. Be sure the computer files you send have your complete name and address in the text. You can send word pro-

March 31, 1997

Susan R. Johnson
1540 Stone River
Whitfield, CA 94616

Clermont County Courthouse
76 South Riverside
Batavia, OH 45103

Dear Sir or Madam:

I would like to order a copy of the following record of marriage.

   George CASTEEL to Rebecca WHITE
   Clermont County, Ohio
   10 June 1824

Please inform me of the cost. I have enclosed a SASE for your convenience.

Thank you very much for your time and attention.

                     Sincerely,

                     Susan R. Johnson
                     Susan R. Johnson

ENC: SASE

Figure 5-6: Sample Request Letter Notice how brief and direct this letter is—the person who fulfills your request will appreciate it! This researcher has avoided the cardinal sins of the amateur genealogist by limiting her request to one record and offering payment. If you prefer, you can call in advance for the current fees, eliminating one step in the process. Don't go fishing in a request letter—always ask for something you can reasonably expect to be there. And leave out those fascinating but completely irrelevant ancestor stories! Finally, remember that SASE (self-addressed, stamped envelope). It's an absolute *necessity*.

cessor files, image files and output files from your genealogy software program. Just be sure to tell your recipient in the body of your E-mail message the name of the software program and its version number.

For correspondents who've never met you, your letter is *you* to them. If it's sloppy and on ragged spiral notebook paper, it makes a statement. A negative statement. And genealogical correspondence tends to hang around for years. Your letter might end up in a manuscript collection one hundred years from now. Remember when your mother told you not to go out without wearing clean underwear in case you had a wreck? Well, don't send out a poorly presented letter in case it should live on in some library's files.

If you have questions about writing business letters, consult a work such as William A. Sabin's *The Gregg Reference Manual*, published by Glencoe McGraw-Hill Book Company. There are many good reference works on this topic.

Keep copies of the letters you send. Even if you're handwriting them, you can slip a piece of carbon paper between two sheets of writing paper. If you're producing them on a word processor or computer, you can easily print two copies—one to mail and one to file. You might also photocopy your letters to produce file copies. You can save your computer-generated letters on disk, but a paper backup copy is a good idea.

When the reply to your letter comes in, you can attach the copy of your letter to it. If you're using E-mail, you may want to print both your message and the response and keep paper copies of your important electronic correspondence. If the letter you receive is a fax, printed on thermal paper, you may want to photocopy it onto plain paper, as thermal paper is an impermanent medium.

There is no free lunch. Offer to pay for the information you receive. Libraries and other repositories may have a policy that sets fees for answering letters and for photocopies supplied with those responses. Many state archives charge research fees to answer letters, especially for out-of-state requests. It is appropriate to write an initial letter to a repository asking about their policy for answering letters requesting genealogical information. If you ask a cousin to send you copies of family photos, offer to pay for copies and postage. Most genealogists exchanging family information expect to be reimbursed only for actual expenses. If, however, you ask a professional genealogist for information, expect to pay for the time involved, too. Have a clear understanding in advance with any professionals about how much your request will cost.

Sending cash through the mail isn't a good idea. Always pay with a personal check, money order or, when possible, a credit card. Don't send payment until you're sure of the amount and your payee.

Except for letters to federal government agencies, always include a self-addressed, stamped envelope (SASE). Use a long, #10, business-sized envelope. Your mailing address should be clearly written on it, and you should affix a first-class postage stamp. Open the flap of the envelope, then fold it in thirds to enclose with your letter. Opening the flap before you fold it makes it a bit less bulky and less apt to have a serious, negative encounter with postal service sorting equipment. Some genealogists use a smaller envelope, a #9, and enclose it without folding in their standard business envelope. One school of thought is that bulky envelopes containing an SASE can be avoided altogether by sending a postage stamp and a return mailing label with your letter. The point is that if you're asking for information and expecting a reply, you should make it easy for that reply to come back to you.

If you're writing to a foreign country, enclosing U.S. postage stamps is of no use. Instead, include International Reply Coupons, which are available from your post office. They can be exchanged by your recipient for appropriate postage.

Faxing Inquiries

Those who own or have easy access to a private fax machine may send inquiries via fax. How do you send a SASE with a faxed inquiry? You can't, of course. You *can* offer to pay for the fax phone call, but a one- or two-page fax usually costs less than a postage stamp and the amount is too small to keep track of. So don't ask for a faxed response unless you can pay for the service in some way. Do put your fax number on your letter so your recipient can respond that way if she chooses. Many agencies who receive a lot of requests for the same information have set up "fax back" systems that let you call their number from your fax machine phone and choose information from an automated menu. The documents then crawl out of your fax machine at your expense. If you use a commercial faxing service (such as your local copy shop), sending and receiving faxes may be more complicated—and expensive.

E-Mail

Electronic mail messages come with a built-in SASE. You just hit the "reply" button. If you're just getting into genealogy and aren't connected to the Internet, give some *very* serious thought to this wonderful, efficient method of correspondence. If you have a personal computer equipped with a modem, you're just a few steps away from an Internet connection. If you subscribe to any computer publications or have ordered software through mail order, you're probably receiving free disks or CD-ROMs from online services or Internet providers on a weekly basis offering "free" trials.

If you aren't a computer owner, call your local library and ask about Internet use. Chances are, you can explore online resources and also set up an E-mail address at the library. If using a computer sounds as alien to you as flying an ultralight airplane, it's time for you to take a class at a local adult education center or community college. In basic computing, not flying. You may be able to purchase a previous-generation, used computer perfectly adequate for your needs at a real bargain. Check with computer-savvy friends for help with finding a used computer.

All the tips about genealogical correspondence that apply to letters also apply to E-mail messages. Be sure your complete return address is included in the E-mail messages you send. It's a bit frustrating to answer messages from Gargoyle@scary.net and never know who your correspondent is. Some E-mail programs let you set up a "signature," a block of text usually containing your full name, mailing address and phone and fax numbers, that will be automatically added to every message you send.

When you write letters and post inquiries, you naturally include your return address. But what if you move? The postal service only forwards mail for one year. Genealogical information hangs around for a long time. It isn't unusual for someone to respond to an inquiry published ten years ago in a genealogical periodical. If you anticipate moving, even in the distant future, consider adding an additional contact address at the end of your letters—perhaps your parents' address or the address of a friend whose feet are firmly planted.

E-mail addresses change even more often than physical addresses. There are several sites on the Internet that allow you to register and list information about yourself, including old and new E-mail addresses.

Several sites on the Internet have posted nationwide business and residential telephone directory information. If you lose track of a cousin, you may be able to search the directory for a new address—*if* the cousin doesn't have a common name. (Common names make everything more difficult in genealogy because you're used to using names to differentiate people. When you encounter several people with the same name, you are forced to search for other identifiers.)

Go Ahead—Get Started

The genealogical record-keeping system I have described here works for most people. It isn't form-intensive or tied to a complicated numbering system. But if it doesn't suit your needs, change it. Many genealogical vendors offer organizing systems and forms.

Start now and create a group sheet for your immediate family. You can do it.

BRANCHING OUT

Beginning Research in Libraries and Archives

At some point in your genealogical quest, you're going to run out of sources in the possession of your family members. And you're going to run out of living family members who can contribute information. Exhaust all those home sources and knowledgeable relatives first. Study and organize everything you find and are told. Analyze the information carefully. Then it's time to broaden your search into libraries.

The first stage of your broadened search should include finding previously unknown cousins who are working on the same family lines you're interested in, and information about your family lines published in books or periodicals. The second stage of research involves finding original records and making your own analysis and evaluation of those materials.

The two stages actually overlap. You may have to do some research in census and other original records to extend your information far enough back in time to connect to printed family histories. And after you discover new family lines, you'll need to search for more researchers and printed materials.

As you do research in libraries, remember to maintain a research calendar like the one described in "Step 5, A Place for Everything: Keeping Records," page 30.

Searching for Published Family Histories

Historians call the initial search for previously published books and articles on a subject a "survey of the literature." You might call it prevention against reinventing the wheel. If some distant cousin has done diligent research and carefully constructed a pedigree, that work could save you

RECORD

OF THE

RUST FAMILY

EMBRACING THE

DESCENDANTS OF HENRY RUST, WHO CAME FROM ENGLAND AND SETTLED IN HINGHAM, MASS., 1634–1635.

Public Library

By ALBERT D. RUST

Dallas, Texas

"HE THAT WISHES TO BE COUNTED AMONG THE BENEFACTORS OF POSTERITY
MUST ADD BY HIS OWN TOIL TO THE ACQUISITIONS OF HIS ANCESTRY."—RAMBLER.

THOROUGHLY INDEXED.

PUBLISHED BY THE AUTHOR:
WACO, TEXAS.
1891.

Figure 6-1: Title Page and Biographical Entry From a Published Family History

149 Thomas Adams[7] (*Jacob Parsons,*[6] *Henry,*[5] *John,*[4] *John,*[3] *Nathaniel,*[2] *Henry*[1]) was born in Salem, 15 Jan., 1798; married first, in Richmond, Va., by Rev. Daniel Roper, 13 May, 1823, Abbie L. Williams, born 26 Feb., 1799; died 8 Oct., 1837; married second, in Richmond, Va., 29 Mar., 1839, by Rev. James B. Taylor, Harriet Willis, daughter of Reuben and Mary Freeman, born 27 Sept., 1817; died 5 Mar., 1844; married third, in Boston, by Rev. R. C. Waterson, 12 May, 1845, Phebe Cutler, daughter of Ephraim and Lydia (Leonard) Chamberlin, of Centre Harbor, N. H., born in Centre Harbor, 11 Sept., 1824. He died at Richmond, Va., 16 Jan., 1882. He was a hardware merchant.

Their children were:

i   Mary Frances,[8] b. 15 June, 1827; d. 27 May, 1829.

ii   Cornelia Lathrop, b. 25 Jan., 1831; m. in Richmond, Va., by Rev. Moses Hodge, 3 Oct., 1850, Woodbury B. Bigelow, b. 5 Oct., 1829. Mr. Bigelow was bookkeeper and Notary Public in and for the State Bank, of Richmond, for eighteen years since the war. He was with the old Farmers' Bank, of Va., thirteen years before the war. He d. 3 Oct., 1888, on the 38th anniversary of his wedding. He was a member of the order A. F. and A. M.; wid. res. 221 S. 3d st., Richmond. They had: i ARCHIBALD BLAIR,[9] (Bigelow) b. 25 July, 1851; m. by Rev. Dr. William Jandrain, 15 Nov., 1887, Miss Blanche Bargamire, of Richmond. He is a bookkeeper. ii MARY WILLIAMS, b. 14 Sept., 1856; m. by Rev. Dr. Moses Hodge, 26 Apr., 1876, Chester A. Delancy. They had: 1 *Josephine.*[10] (Delancy) 2 *Mamie.* 3 *Nellie.* iii WILLIAM M., (Bigelow) b. 15 Aug., 1860. He is a rapid and correct calculator; is entry clerk for a large wholesale house in Richmond; res. 221 South third street.

iii Thomas, b. 15 Oct., 1833; d. 13 Sept., 1834.

iv   Sarah Ann, b. 3 Sept., 1836; d. 21 Jan., 1837.

          (The above are children of first wife.)

v   Henry Freeman, b. 29 Jan., 1840; d. 10 Jan., 1873.

vi   Charles Francis, b. 24 June, 1841; d. 31 July, 1843.

285 vii Edward Freeman, b. 31 Jan., 1843; m. Julia Cabell.

          (The above are children of second wife.)

286 viii Charles Manning b. 12 Feb., 1846; m. Mary L. Wood.

ix   Annie Cooledge, b. 12 Nov., 1847.

This entry from a published family history is a gold mine of information for the genealogist. But remember: Just because it appears in print doesn't mean it's true. Always verify your information with original source documents.

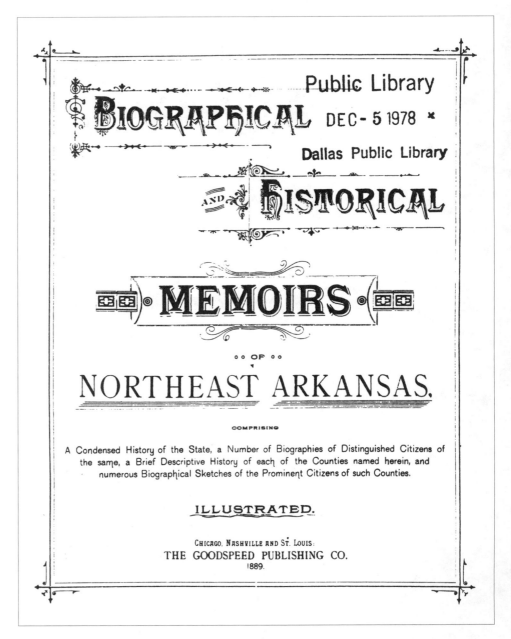

Figure 6-2: County "Mugbooks" Another resource for the genealogist is the published county history, or "mugbook." These books, commonly printed in the 1880s and 1890s, contained not only the history of a county, but biographies of some of its residents. Newton L. Hamm, the subject of this entry, became a "noted resident of Izard County, Arkansas" by paying for the honor, but the real payoff is to his descendants. Newton Hamm's birthdate and birthplace indicate to the genealogist where to seek census records for clues to *Newton's* ancestors. He owned land, so the researcher knows to check Izard County deed books. The mini-biography even spells out the maiden name of Newton's wife and gives her religious affiliation; the genealogist can now trace *her* family with church records. Further avenues for pursuit? Newton's church, his Masonic lodge, and his children.

946   HISTORY OF ARKANSAS.

Newton L. Hamm. The estate which Mr. Hamm is now engaged in cultivating embraces 266 acres of land, which are well adapted to the purposes of general farming, and in his operations he displays those sterling principles which are characteristic of those of Tennessee birth, industry, and wise and judicious management being chief among the number. He has 150 acres of his land under cultivation, it being well improved with good buildings, fences, etc., and stocked with all the necessary farm animals for successfully conducting the same. He was born in McNairy County, June 24, 1840, and is one of five surviving members of a family of ten sons and seven daughters, born to William and Rachel (Huggins) Hamm, both of whom were born on Blue Grass soil, the former's birth occurring on the 20th of October, 1799, and the latter's September 13, 1798. They were tillers of the soil, and at the time of the father's death, December 10, 1872, he was the owner of 120 acres of land. He had attained a high rank in the Masonic lodge, having been a member of that organization from the time he was twenty-one years of age, and also belonged to the Hard Shell Baptist Church. He was followed to his long home by his wife on the 10th of January, 1874. Newton L. Hamm's youth was spent in attending the common schools of Tennessee, and in assisting his father on the home farm. In 1855 he moved to Arkansas, and was married here on the 1st of November, 1863, to Miss Nettie Frizzell, she having been born in Henry County, Tenn., and a daughter of Jason and Mahala Frizzell, and ten children have blessed their union, nine of whom, still living, reside at home with their parents: Carrol, William, Asa, Emmer, Joseph, Jason, Philip, Newton, Leroy and Adah E. In 1862 he enlisted in the Confederate army under Gen. Hindman, and was at the battle of Prairie Grove. He was discharged at the surrender of Jacksonport. Like his father he is a Mason, and he is a member of the Baptist Church, his wife being a member of the Methodist Church.

F. M. Hanley, attorney, Melbourne, Ark. Prominent among the comparatively young men of Izard County, Ark., whose career thus far has been both honorable and successful, is the subject of this present sketch. He was born in Graves County, Ky., in 1845, and his parents, F. M. and Elizabeth (Mobley) Hanley, were also natives of the Blue Grass State. The parents were married about 1838, and the father was a successful agriculturist in his native State. He died in 1845, and the mother died in 1854. Both were members of the Methodist Episcopal Church, and he was Democratic in his views. Their family consisted of five children, three now living: James E. (resides in Kentucky, and follows farming), Mary E. (wife of Joseph G. Henry, and resides in Kentucky), and F. M. The paternal grandfather was born in Tipperary, Ireland, and came to America when quite a young man. The paternal grandmother was also a native of the Emerald Isle. The maternal grandparents were natives of Ireland, and were married there before coming to America. F. M. Hanley was left an orphan when quite young, and, at the age of nine years, he was taken to Todd County, Ky., and bound out to Johnston Carr. He was reared on a farm, attending the subscription schools of his county until his fifteenth year, after which he entered the St. Joseph College, at Bardstown, and there remained two years. When seventeen years of age he enlisted in the Confederate army, Company D, Second Kentucky Infantry Regiment, and served until the 7th of May, 1865, participating in the following battles: Fort Donelson, Hartsville, Murfreesboro, Jackson, Chickamauga and Missionary Ridge, and was in all the battles from Resaca to Jonesboro, where he was captured, on the 1st of September, 1864, but was retained only a short time. Previous to this he was captured at Fort Donelson, and was retained by the United States forces from February to September, 1862. After being exchanged the last time his command was mounted. Upon coming home he attended school at Spring Grove Academy, Todd County, Ky., and subsequently spent three years "teaching the young idea" and in studying law, under Williams, Turner & Williams. He was admitted to the bar, at Mayfield, Ky., in 1869, and engaged in the practice of his profession at that place. In 1873 he came to Phillips County, Ark.,

years of finding all that information yourself. But just because you find something in print about your ancestors doesn't mean it's true. You'll still need to examine original records to verify what you read, but previous research can be very helpful.

Libraries are not only a source of published genealogies and genealogical periodicals, they also house volumes of compiled census indexes and transcriptions, cemetery inventories, books about local history, and many other reference sources essential to genealogists. Archives, on the other hand, are usually repositories for retired official records of public or private agencies. Sometimes, archives also have collections of the same types of books found in libraries. And some libraries maintain collections of manuscript materials and thus function much like archives.

Some libraries specialize in genealogical research materials. The reference department of most libraries has two especially helpful library directories that will tell you about these genealogy libraries. The R.R. Bowker Co. publishes *American Library Directory* annually, and it lists thousands of libraries in the U.S. and Canada, including those with genealogical collections. Gale Research Co. publishes *A Directory of Special Libraries and Information Centers*, which identifies libraries with especially large genealogy departments. Check with your local library's reference librarian to learn more about these directories.

The largest genealogical library in the world is the Family History Library in Salt Lake City, Utah. The library, owned by the Church of Jesus Christ of Latter-day Saints (LDS or Mormons), was founded in 1894 and contains information about families from all over the world. Databases with millions of entries on deceased people are available through the Family History Library. In addition to collecting a tremendous number of published materials, the Mormons have gone throughout the world, microfilming original records. They've done this so genealogists like you will have access to these records without making long, expensive trips to the places where the records are kept. However, they couldn't copy everything, and you may eventually find yourself making a trip to that ancestral homeland to search for records. But you'll have a head start in the records microfilmed by the Mormons.

Many of the resources of the Family History Library are available through a branch library system set up in local LDS churches. These are called Family History Centers and can be located by checking local telephone directories for "Church of Jesus Christ of Latter-day Saints," then calling to inquire about the nearest Family History Center. The centers, staffed by volunteers, are usually open on a limited basis, so it's best to call and ask about operating hours before planning a visit. The Family History Library can also supply information over the phone or on their Web site about the location of Family History Centers, their telephone numbers and operating hours. Check the Resources section (Appendix B) for more information.

Published Family Histories

One part of the library catalog for the Family History Library is devoted to family histories published through the years by genealogists who've compiled the results of their research. The Family History Library has made an effort to collect as many published genealogies as possible. Their holdings of family histories range from small booklets to giant volumes, from amateur's work to that of renowned professionals. All the Family

History Centers have the complete library catalog on microfiche and CD-ROM. After you locate a specific title about your family, you can take steps to borrow a copy. You may be able to borrow a microfilmed copy from the Family History Library. Or you might request photocopies of the index pages of a family history to see if you recognize any of the names. If so, you can submit a request for photocopies of the chapters of the book that interest you.

The Library of Congress in Washington, DC, has thousands of published genealogies in its massive collection. You can search its catalog online through the Internet to learn about books on your family lines. Bibliographies of family histories in the Library of Congress collection have been published.

If you only know the names of your ancestors as far back as your grandparents, you may not readily find a published family history unless one of your cousins has written one. But as you learn more about your family and discover more and more distant ancestors, the likelihood of finding a published genealogy greatly increases. This phase of searching for published family histories should be repeated every time you discover a new family line or a new set of grandparents.

Remember, just because it's in print doesn't make it so. When you do find a published family history, don't take its contents on faith. And don't let a fancy cover and many reproduced original documents fool you. The author of that volume, no matter how famous and accomplished, may have misinterpreted the information. And, if the book was written many years ago, new indexes to source documents may turn up evidence not accessible when the book was written.

Searching for Published Articles About Your Family

A tremendous amount of genealogical information has been published in historical and genealogical periodicals. Local historical societies, genealogy clubs, family associations and ethnic-specific organizations have published thousands of journals, newsletters, magazines and quarterlies. Some of these periodicals are indexed in each issue, some annually, and a few have cumulative indexes that cover several years. But it's very tedious to figure out which journal might contain an article about your family, then locate back issues in a library so you can make a trip to the library and go through the indexes. There's a better way.

The Allen County Public Library in Fort Wayne, Indiana, began a massive indexing project of genealogical periodicals in 1987. They called this project PERSI for *PERiodical Source Index*. Staff members began indexing articles for the previous year, then continued, producing annual index volumes. In addition, they began indexing older material and created a 16-volume retrospective index to over 4,100 publications. It gets better. In

1997, this enormous database was published by Ancestry, Inc., a genealogical commercial vendor, on one CD-ROM.

PERSI is divided into five subject categories: U.S., Canadian, and foreign place names, research methodology, and family records. It's a *subject* index, not an every-name index. So an article about the Smith family that contains mention of your Abner Jones would only list the name "Smith" in PERSI. But if the title of the article was "Smith Family of Randolph County, North Carolina, 1776–1835," and you knew your Jones family lived in that area during that time period, you'd probably want to read that article. PERSI is an index only—it doesn't contain the text of the articles. But once you know the periodical name and article title, you can obtain photocopies of the entire article by requesting a copy from the holdings of the Allen County Public Library, the Family History Library, or another library whose collection includes the periodical you need. You might also obtain a copy of a particular article by writing to the organization which published the material.

Not all family history articles have been published in genealogy periodicals. Some are found in publications outside PERSI's scope. You should use traditional periodical finding aids in the reference section of your library to search for family history material in publications not included in PERSI.

Searching for Fellow Researchers

When you begin your survey of the literature on the subject of your family's history, cross your fingers and hope some remote cousin *published* some helpful information. It's easier to find than *unpublished* material. To find the unpublished information, you'll have to search for living cousins who are researching or have worked on discovering your common lineage. These cousins are probably folks you've never met, and you'll discover them as you become a part of the genealogical community.

Genealogists have a lot in common, and when you make contact with a local genealogical or historical society, you'll probably make some really enjoyable friends. These new friends can help you learn about resources and share your enthusiasm about your research.

Queries

Most genealogy groups publish some kind of periodical. One popular topic in these publications is inquiries (called *queries*) from researchers seeking help on particular families. It's like a dating service, only the object is a bit different—it's an *ancestor* match you're after. If the area where you live has a genealogical society, you can benefit from membership even though you may not have ancestors from there. And you'll also probably

EDWARDS

Seeking parents and siblings for Jeremiah A. ROBERTSON (ca 1823 VA-1871, Hardin, KY) who md. Susannah SWOPES (ca 1829, KY-abt 1855, Hardin, KY). Children: Ambrose (1847), Femy (1849), Jeremiah A. (1852), and Samuell (1855). #Rosene Robertson, 1396 Oak Park Drive, Topeka, KS 66614 (rosen@ixcom.net).

want to join the groups in places where your ancestors lived for long periods of time. Dues are inexpensive and usually entitle you to place queries in their publication.

To locate the addresses of genealogical societies, check Elizabeth Petty Bentley's *The Genealogist's Address Book*, published by Genealogical Publishing Co., Inc. in Baltimore. The reference section of your local library may have a copy of this directory. The American Association for State and Local History also publishes a directory that includes historical societies and museums. In addition, many organizations are establishing informational Web sites on the Internet.

Other than through genealogy groups, you may find cousins directly through mail lists and newsgroups on the Internet. If you participate, read the messages posted to the group for a while to get a "feel" for how to place your inquiries about your research needs. To learn more about mail lists, newsgroups and Internet sources specific to genealogy, read Cyndi Howells's *Netting Your Ancestors: Genealogical Research on the Internet* and Richard S. Wilson and Barbara Renick's *The Internet for Genealogists: A Beginner's Guide*.

Before you place a query in a society's periodical, study the ones published in recent issues. An inquiry about a specific family in a particular place during a certain time period is best. Give full names of the people you're interested in as well as where they lived, and mention the time frame. Be specific about what you want to know.

Follow whatever rules and policies are established by the society board members or the publication's editor when placing a query in their periodical. In general, don't abbreviate anything—the person who edits the query for publication will apply a standard set of abbreviations.

Queries aren't limited to those published in periodicals. They can take the form of note cards posted on courthouse bulletin boards (with permission, of course). Or business cards printed with your ancestral lines. One researcher left a note in a marriage record volume in a courthouse, stuck in the pages where her ancestor's marriage was recorded. The note said,

"If you're related to Bart Abernathy, call me at (and she included her phone number)." She did this in several courthouses, always being careful to use acid-free paper and penciled notes that wouldn't damage the records. So far, she's had two calls from people who read her notes. One was from a previously unknown cousin, the other from a fellow genealogist who just wanted to tell her how creative she thought the idea was.

A major genealogical software vendor is soliciting family history data files from the users of its programs to include on CD-ROMs. These compilations of family trees are then sold as commercial products. They're actually a form of query. People can contribute as much or as little of their information as they choose. They include their names and addresses so people who are potential relatives can contact them. Many success stories have come from this project. If you're in the position of deciding whether to participate in this project or one like it, think of it as a way to contact cousins and share some of your information. It's like dangling a little fish bait in the genealogical waters.

This system of placing queries, however you do it, to find fellow researchers is based on a mutual sharing of information. While you may have only started your research, some distant cousin may be interested in information on your immediate branch of the family and be willing to help you with the distant ancestor you have in common.

What you'll be sharing with cousins is *information*, and the easiest way to transmit that is with well-documented family group sheets, either on paper or as computer files. Your pedigree chart will also be helpful to show someone your lineage. If you want to be respected as a thorough, competent researcher, include mention of all your sources on your family group sheets. Show where each data item came from. If your correspondents want copies of any of your original materials, they'll ask.

Queries hang around for a long time. One researcher answered a query that was twenty-six years old. Read about her experience in the accompanying sidebar.

When you receive material from other researchers, ask where they got their information, if they don't tell you initially. If they can't supply citations, then use their data with great caution. If you incorporate their family information with your own, you'll have to cite the person who gave you the data as the source. Now think about it; the living cousin who says Great-grandfather was born in 1875 wasn't an eyewitness, was she? So if she wasn't present, how does she know? Perhaps she copied the date from a gravestone, read it on a death certificate, computed it from his age listed in a federal census record or found it in the family Bible. Ask *how* she knows.

Even if you're supplied with undocumented information, you can still use it as research clues. Your source (until you confirm it in other records) is the person who told you or supplied you with the facts.

In addition to exchanging information, you can exchange photos with newly found cousins. They may have photos of your ancestors which have

OLD QUERIES NEVER DIE

Leslie is an unusual woman, and she uses some unusual genealogical methods in her research. Much to the astonishment of her friends, they usually pay off. Here's Leslie's story about answering a very old query:

"After chasing my great-great-grandpa for a roller-coaster six months, I ran into a brick wall. Was there nothing more I could do? Was I doomed to have ancestry that stopped in 1854?

"Hardly—because old queries never die. Thumbing through periodicals on the state in which my family had lived, I stumbled across a query on my very own ancestor, a query printed twenty-six years before. In the great scheme of things, twenty-six years is only an instant, I reasoned. I cautiously checked a telephone directory for the town where the long-ago submitter lived (and it was a fairly small town). No surprise there—there was no listing for the name at the address in the query. There was, however, one current listing for that surname in the town, though the first name was different. So I took the plunge and responded to that twenty-six-year-old query to a different person at a different address.

"To my astonishment, it worked. Two weeks after I wrote, I received a response from the daughter of the query's author. My letter had gone to her sister-in-law, who had sent it on to her. Her father, she said, was a fearsome genealogist who had pursued our ancestor until the very end of his days. He'd left a wealth of papers to his nongenealogist daughter. She was at a loss as to what to do with them, how to organize the material or whether to pitch the whole mess.

"Thrilled that someone was interested, she promptly invited me to visit. I spent a glorious day wallowing in the research files of a cousin whom I'll never meet. Several hours at a copy shop later, I had a ream of information and a Revolutionary War ancestor—one who received a pension, at that. I came away with a copy of an original will that had come down through my newly found cousin's branch of the family. I had information on wives and children in other, related lines, and I had an old list of his correspondents, one of whom I still write to today.

"I've been back to visit several more times. Inexplicably, my new cousin still doesn't do genealogical research, but I've helped her organize the files and arrange to donate them to the genealogy library nearest the family home. I've tried, in part, to repay her father for the help he unknowingly gave me.

"Since then, I've become even more creative about pursuing cold trails. I shamelessly write letters to the editors of small-town newspapers in locations where people in whom I'm interested were reported on the 1920 census. I telephone total strangers who have familiar names in areas where my ancestors lived. I appeal to employees in cemetery and funeral home offices for information on deceased distant relatives in the hope they'll help me contact the living family members who made the final arrangements. I order death certificates and copies of obituaries of people from whom I'm not descended just to get the names of the living survivors. And all of these radical behaviors have paid off."

For a genealogist, no trail is too faint to follow.

been lost to your branch of the family. And they'll probably want photos of you and your family. It's interesting to look for common physical characteristics. Share *copies* of your old photos, not the originals. New color photocopiers available today produce quick, near-photo-quality images of your old pictures. You can also share computer image files made from scanned photos. Photo image files can be attached to electronic mail messages and sent through the Internet.

Remember to label the photos you share. You can write on the backs of traditional resin-coated photo paper with a very soft lead pencil. Record the names of the people or subject of the photo, the date the photo was taken, and your name as the supplier of the photo. If you send copies made on a photocopier, label a scrap of paper with identifying information and photocopy it onto the same sheet of paper as the photo. If you scan a photo to make an image file, attach a label at the bottom of the photo and scan the label as part of the image so it'll be permanently attached.

Looking in Libraries

After you've assembled and analyzed all the sources you can find in your family's possession, seek published books and articles about your family. Then pursue genealogists who are working on your family lines. Once found, exchange information with them. But eventually, you'll reach a stopping point—no more help from fellow researchers, nothing else written about your folks. It's time to direct your search into original records.

You've already encountered original records—remember the birth, marriage and death certificates you either found at home or wrote for? The cemeteries you visited where your family members are buried contain original records of a sort. Original records tell us about the events themselves, and it's up to us to examine, evaluate and analyze those records, then use them to assemble our lineages. We must develop an ear for listening to the documents that may tell us about our ancestors.

Before you go further afield in search of original records, it's a good idea to search library sources for published transcriptions, abstracts and indexes to original records—sometimes called secondary sources.

You begin your search for published secondary sources by looking at your family information. Where did they live? The records you need are specific to particular geographic locations. In order to begin research in federal census records, you have to know at least the state in which the family lived during a year the census was taken. To find marriage records, you must guess the county where the marriage took place.

If you create a chronology for your immediate family, you might see many places involved. Perhaps you were born in one place, grew up in another, went away to college, met your future spouse (who was from somewhere else), returned home to marry, but then you both moved to a faraway place to accept promising jobs. You had children along the way. Your career choices had a lot to do with where you lived. Eventually, you and your spouse built up enough seniority on your jobs to get transferred to a place you wanted to live. Your kids left for college. Retirement planning began, and you bought property in a warm climate. You moved again when retirement came.

Think about how many different places have records about you and your nuclear family. Birth certificates, school transcripts, college diplomas, marriage licenses, rental agreements, deed records, children's birth certificates, employment records, telephone directories, more deed records, tax records, auto and drivers' licenses, Elvis fan club membership cards, insurance policies, vacation mementos and dozens of other records about you exist in your home and in public places. If you changed spouses, sued someone, ran afoul of the law or did something newsworthy, you generated even more records.

Even though we're a much more mobile society today, it's the same story for your ancestral families. The records they left are different, but you use them just the same to piece together pictures of their lives.

Don't forget about those groups of people who are also involved with your family; those allied and associated families who were also creating records. Just as your life has touched the lives of others in a wide variety of ways, so did your ancestors' lives.

All of these events in your life and the lives of your ancestors happened in specific geographic places. You must identify these places in order to search for records. You need maps, gazetteers and atlases to help with your search for place names.

Maps for Genealogists

Locating place names can be a real challenge for genealogists. One of the most useful databases of U.S. place names was created by United States Geological Survey (USGS). It's called the Geographic Names Information System (GNIS). Employees and contractors entered all the place names from USGS's most detailed kind of maps, the 7.5-minute topographic maps. They didn't just enter towns, they keyed in all natural features— hills, mountains, streams, rivers, creeks, valleys, knobs, lakes and others— that had a name. They entered every school, cemetery, crossroads, village, town, city, populated place and any other manmade feature found on the maps. Then, in phase two of the project, they began to enter place names from old sources, creating a very helpful source for genealogists.

Each entry in the GNIS database lists the place name, its "feature class" (populated place, cemetery, school, lake, stream, etc.), county, geographic coordinate (longitude and latitude description), source coordinate, elevation and name of the 7.5-minute topographic map on which the place appears.

The GNIS database is available for searches on the Internet. It's sold on CD-ROM as a USGS product. (See "Maps" in the Resources section of this book.) Paper printouts for selected states are available, and it's available on microfiche. It's much better to use GNIS in electronic form, because you can pull up all the cemeteries in Rowan County, North Carolina, or all the places in the United States named "Walnut Bottom," or all the watercourses in Smith County, Tennessee.

Other lists of place names, called "gazetteers," are available for a wide range of regions and time periods. *Omni Gazetteer of the United States of America*, an 11-volume set published by Omnigraphics, is a comprehensive reference tool found in many libraries.

Maps of all descriptions are good research aids for genealogists. One of the most useful and widely available are county maps. Most state highway departments sell county maps for their states, sometimes in two scales. The small-scale county maps are ideal to take along on research trips; the large ones allow enough space to write in ancestral landholdings. Most maps from state agencies are inexpensive. (See the Resources section under "Maps" for a helpful booklet, *Where to Write for County Maps.*) Most of the state mapping agencies or tourism offices offer free highway maps of their states.

Some state mapping agencies have reprinted old maps of their state. Indiana offers an especially nice variety of old map reprints. Alabama's "Old Roads and Traces" map is very helpful. Some state mapping agencies sell copies of older versions of their county maps. When you write to inquire about price, always ask about reprints of older maps.

Before you order county maps, remember that county boundaries have changed through the years. In 1820, Madison County, Illinois, covered much of the western part of the state. Today, it occupies just a very small area at the southern end of its 1820 boundaries. The best reference source on this subject is William Thorndale and William Dollarhide's *Map Guide to the U.S. Federal Censuses, 1790-1920.*

USGS produces a variety of maps. The most detailed are 7.5-minute topographic maps—the ones they used to prepare the GNIS database. These maps show a wonderful level of detail, including relief lines which illustrate elevation. They're inexpensive and available for every area of the United States. Each map covers a small land area, so it usually takes several 7.5 topographic maps to cover a county. Many genealogists, however, can pinpoint the area where their ancestors lived (from deeds and other land records) and may need only one or two to cover the area they're interested in.

To find the particular USGS maps you want, you need two booklets for each state of interest. The booklets, a map catalog and a map index, are available free from USGS. You can order them by calling USGS's toll-free request line: (800) USA-MAPS. You'll be talking to a machine, so speak slowly and *very* clearly. When the booklets arrive, read the introductory information to learn about map scales and ordering information.

You don't have to order the maps in their catalog directly from USGS. They're available from many sources. State mapping agencies often stock them for their states. Hiking shops usually carry them for their areas; commercial map shops stock them. Ordering from USGS with a credit card is probably the easiest way to get the maps if they aren't available locally.

If you're interested in old maps, you have some alternatives. You can buy originals from dealers who specialize in old, rare maps. You can buy reprints of old maps from genealogical vendors who advertise regularly in periodicals such as *Heritage Quest* and *Everton's Genealogical Helper*. And you can visit libraries and archives that have old maps among their holdings. To locate information about map collections, consult David A. Cobb's *Guide to US Map Resources*, published by the American Library Association.

To learn more about all kinds of maps, including those produced by commercial companies, read *The Map Catalog: Every Kind of Map and Chart on Earth and Even Some Above It, Third Ed.* by Joel Makower.

The National Archives has a tremendous map collection. It doesn't produce maps; it just holds, catalogs and preserves maps created by a wide variety of federal sources, including USGS. There are a number of preliminary inventories, special lists, catalogs and unpublished finding aids that describe some of the map holdings of the National Archives' Cartographic and Architectural Branch. The maps held by the National Archives include those generated by exploration, public land surveys, Indian affairs, navigation, agriculture, topography and natural resources, census mapping, military campaigns and more. A starting point for the National Archives' most popular maps is *Special List 29: List of Selected Maps of States and Territories*, a resource originally prepared by National Archives staff members, but now available from a commercial source.

The Library of Congress in Washington, DC, has a tremendous collection of maps. Much of their catalog is online and available through the Internet. The library catalog contains descriptions of the maps, not images of the maps themselves.

Commercial mapping companies have published street maps for the entire United States on CD-ROM. With these it's possible to enter a zip code, telephone area code or street name and quickly view a map of the area.

Maps are helpful for genealogists who want to find a geographic location, but they're also valuable from another standpoint. Maps help us visualize the territory where our ancestors lived. With maps we can see surrounding political jurisdictions. When we can't locate a marriage record for an ancestor, we can look at a map and make an educated guess about where that ancestral couple might have gone. Maps help us visualize physical features as well. If a range of mountains separated our ancestors from the area to which they were migrating, we can look at a map and see the route they may have taken around the barrier. When travel was primarily on waterways, maps show us these routes.

County Boundary Changes

Identify the places where your ancestors lived. Use maps and gazetteers to find those locations mentioned in your records. Investigate to learn what the political jurisdiction was during the time period your ancestors lived in that place. *The Handy Book for Genealogists* published by Everton Publishers lists all the counties in all the states and gives their creation dates and a description of the territory from which they were created. (The equivalent of counties are called parishes in Louisiana.) The book lists the county seats and mailing addresses of the courthouses. It gives very brief descriptions of the starting dates of major record groups. Capsule histories of the states and brief bibliographies of reference material give you a starting place for research. Thorndale and Dollarhide's *Map Guide to the U.S. Federal Censuses, 1790–1920* presents much of the same information in a graphic format.

In an ideal situation, you should visit the state archives and a major genealogical library in the state where your ancestors lived. Then you should explore the courthouse where your folks went to transact day-to-day business, and you should stop by the local library to examine any records specific to that area. In reality, unless you're very fortunate, you can't do this for all the states where your ancestors lived. Earning a living and family responsibilities have a way of intervening in your genealogical research. What are you going to do?

Finding Secondary Sources

Your research efforts may start with the materials available at your local library or the nearest library with a genealogical collection. Then you have to expand your search for secondary sources about the *places* where your ancestors lived. Visit LDS Family History Centers and seek out libraries within driving distance that have genealogical collections.

Many county histories have been written through the years. During the late 1800s, some companies compiled county histories and included biographical sketches of prominent local citizens. These were often published in regional volumes. They've been reprinted in recent times as genealogical interest in them grew.

Genealogical societies and individuals have transcribed or compiled indexes to deeds, wills, marriages, tax lists, newspapers, church records, cemeteries and other records. You can locate these books with traditional search methods in library catalogs. Many libraries have posted their catalogs of holdings on the Internet. You can use the keyword search function on most library Web sites to find books about specific places. The problem you'll encounter when searching for these kinds of sources is that they were usually published in very small press runs and had a limited distribution. The Family History Library in Salt Lake City has made a special effort to search out and acquire these works. Their catalog lists them in the "locality" listings.

The series, *Genealogical and Local History Books in Print*, now in its fifth edition, offers researchers a way to find many genealogical sources. People who've compiled genealogies and other secondary sources have contributed information about how to purchase their books, but this series can also be used as a way to find those books in libraries. This series is not comprehensive, but it can lead you to books you wouldn't learn about any other way. Most libraries with genealogical reference sections have this series, and the current edition is for sale from Genealogical Publishing Co., Inc. (see "Vendors" in the Resources section).

Secondary, or compiled, sources shouldn't be used *instead of* primary sources. Most compilers advise readers to use their books as finding aids to original records. Secondary sources should never be used to determine that a record *doesn't* exist. When a listing doesn't appear in an index, it means nothing more than you didn't find it in the index. It doesn't even mean the entry wasn't in the index. It may be there, but under a spelling variation you missed. When you don't find an entry for a particular person in a census index, it doesn't mean that person isn't listed in the census records themselves.

Secondary sources are often indexes or lists of names. Be careful that you don't abandon your search for *people* and begin a search for *names*. Maintain your search for groups of people, not just one individual.

Etiquette

When you venture into libraries and archives in search of family information, follow their regulations. In many facilities, you'll be given a list of the rules when you register. Often you'll be required to show identification to obtain a researcher's card. Your personal belongings may be examined before and after you use the library. The rules are in place for a purpose, and your cooperation will expedite your research.

Staff members are often overworked and underpaid. Do ask them for information, but be brief with your questions. Don't tell family stories. If a librarian needs more information about your family in order to point you toward the right resources, she'll ask. When you ask for information, *listen* to the answer. Listen carefully, then ask for clarification if you need it. If you're expected to reshelve the books you use, do so. If you're allowed only five photocopies before returning to the end of the copier line, do only five. If you're directed to use only pencils for writing, use a pencil.

Research time is often limited, especially for people who've driven a long way to use the library. Don't take up your fellow researchers' time with your family stories or extended complaints about library rules or personnel.

Wear appropriate clothing. Though it sounds unfair, your attire can have an impact on your success in a library. Staff members are people, and people often make judgments about others based upon how they're dressed. The person in the business suit may be offered more assistance than the one in shorts and T-shirt.

Remember your manners—say please and thank you, take turns, obey the rules—and you'll have a more pleasant research experience.

STEP 7

YOU CAN'T HAVE ONE WITHOUT THE OTHER
History and Genealogy

Genealogy and history are intertwined. In order to understand your ancestors, you have to learn more about the times and events that surrounded their lives. Without this historical context, genealogy can get pretty dry. A collection of names and dates doesn't explain who your ancestors were.

Reading history can bring your ancestors to life. They were part of the social, economic, religious and political events of their time. There's an added benefit—reading history can help you solve genealogical problems. When you can't find a previous residence for an ancestor, read about the factors that caused migration to the area where you know your ancestor lived. Learn where other people came from and why they came. Chances are, your problem of the previous residence will be solved.

When you begin your genealogy search, you're looking for tiny bits of data, small clues. You only want a single marriage record out of dozens of marriages performed that year in a particular place. You're after the deed records for your great-grandfather, so you sift through hundreds of other land records. Cautioned to look for details, you go about this project with a magnifying glass. Keep on, and you'll miss the big picture.

Step back from your research and use a wide-angle lens. Look at the big picture. See your ancestors as part of something larger. Read about all aspects of history.

A Reading Plan

So many books, so little time. How are you going to pick and choose what you want to read to supplement your genealogy? All genealogists have a common interest in topics like marriage, death, social customs, migration patterns and local history. Beyond the broad topics, though, special interest takes over, and you have to select books about topics that tell you more about your ancestors.

Consider your ancestors' lives. When did they live? Where? If your earliest American ancestor was Irish and came over during the potato famines of the 1840s, you probably aren't interested in colonial American history. Assess the information you have about your family members. Don't just concentrate on the distant past. If your father served in the military during World War II and your mother worked in a defense plant, do some reading about that event. It probably had a major impact on their lives. If they're alive, ask about personal recollections, then supplement those reminiscences with reading.

Your grandparents may have left the Midwest during the Great Depression and migrated to California. Read about those times and learn what caused your ancestors to load up all their belongings and move half a continent away. Historians have written extensively about our past. All you have to do is find the books and articles.

It isn't easy, however; finding materials of interest requires research. If your library's catalog is online, use the keyword search and enter topics of interest. If the catalog is still in paper form, use the subject cards. Check the reference department of your library for *Harvard Guide to American History*, compiled by Frank Freidel. It's a bit dated, but a good place to start. This set contains bibliographies arranged by topic.

Talk with the reference librarian and ask about finding aids—guides for finding books of interest—for humanities subjects. The most commonly used guides are the *Reader's Guide to Periodical Literature* and the *National Union Catalog* (or NUC), which is now online. Your librarian will explain the resources available in your library.

Once you locate a book or article on a subject you're interested in, pay attention to the footnotes and bibliography. An author who does a thorough job tells you about sources for the material used in writing the book. Start a list of books you want to find, based on bibliographies in the volumes you've found. You have been advised to keep a research calendar of the genealogical sources you've searched—you can do the same for history books and articles. And you can list the books and journal articles on that list that you *want* to read, as well.

In the genealogical field, we're lucky to have the *PERiodical Source Index* (PERSI) compiled by the Allen County Public Library in Fort Wayne, Indiana (see the discussion of PERSI in "Step 6: Branching Out, page 53). The only index in the field of history that approaches the comprehensiveness of PERSI is *America: History and Life*, published by ABC-Clio, Inc. It is available on microfiche and CD-ROM at major libraries.

When you find a citation to an article in a historical journal, check to see if your library owns copies of the back issues for that title. If not, talk to the interlibrary loan specialist about ordering a photocopy of the article. Sometimes you're required to pay for photocopies, but often there's no charge for this service.

You can also use interlibrary loan to obtain the history books of interest to you. Ask about your library's policy—sometimes there's a charge for the service. It's often very difficult to find an interlibrary loan source for genealogy books, but history books were published in larger press runs and are more readily available.

A good strategy for reading is to start with a broad overview, then narrow your reading. Begin with a history of the United States. You can scan a high school or college textbook for a refresher course on political history. To learn more about social history, try Daniel J. Boorstin's trilogy about American social history, *The Americans*. The first of the three volumes, *The Americans: The Colonial Experience*, describes life in early America. Boorstin writes about the people—Quakers, Puritans, Virginians—and the kinds of communities they established. He writes about the legal profession, medicine, science, language and books. In the second volume, *The Americans: The National Experience*, he describes New Englanders who made fortunes from granite and ice, the people who migrated westward in such haste, the boosters and the builders who created new communities, and the black and white Southerners. In the third volume, *The Americans: The Democratic Experience*, Boorstin writes about range wars, divorce, gambling, crime, standardized clothing, advertising, food preservation, snake oil remedies, grammar and other social history topics. Best of all, all three volumes contain excellent bibliographical essays that lead you to other sources.

Narrowing Your Focus

After the overview, narrow your focus to the time and place of your ancestors' lives. For example, you might consult the "Everyday Life Series" from Writer's Digest Books. Although written for writers, genealogists find them useful. The series includes Dale Taylor's *The Writer's Guide to Everyday Life in Colonial America*, Marc McCutcheon's *The Writer's Guide to Everyday Life in the 1800s* (America), Kristine Hughes's *The Writer's Guide to Everyday Life in Regency and Victorian England*, and McCutcheon's *The Writer's Guide to Everyday Life From Prohibition Through World War II*.

If your ancestors were among the millions who pushed the American frontier westward, read two books by Ted Morgan, *Wilderness at Dawn: The Settling of the North American Continent* and *A Shovel of Stars: The Making of the American West, 1800 to the Present*. Morgan isn't a professional historian like many writers of history—his works read like adventure tales. His second volume offers great detail about states' territorial periods.

One of the best books on American migrations westward is Ray Allen Billington's *Westward Expansion: A History of the American Frontier*. The book has been through several editions and can be found in libraries and used book stores. It contains a very thorough bibliography, annotated with Billington's comments about the sources.

Your interest may be in a specific ethnic group. If your ancestors are Irish, German, Jewish, Italian, Chinese, Japanese, African-American, Puerto Rican, or Mexican, start with Thomas Sowell's *Ethnic America: A History*. In a wonderfully readable style, he talks about the push-pull factors that brought these groups to the United States. He calls the peopling of America "one of the great dramas of human history."

Then search for more specific books that only deal with the people you're descended from. Probably your ancestors were a mixture of several ethnic groups. Read about them. Read about the political and social history of the countries from which they came.

If your ancestors were Scots-Irish, for example, you might start with *The Scotch-Irish: A Social History* by James G. Leyburn. It's an older work (1962) and paints a picture of these hard-working, industrious people who always managed to be on the edge of civilization. For an alternate view of the same folks, try Grady McWhiney's *Cracker Culture: Celtic Ways in the Old South*. His Scots-Irish were *hardly*-working people who preferred the frontier to get away from governmental interference.

Move your reading from the particular ethnic group to the time and place where they settled. Robert W. Ramsey's *Carolina Cradle: Settlement of the Northwest Carolina Frontier, 1747-1762* describes not only the Scots-Irish, but also the other ethnic groups with whom they came into contact in the backwoods.

If you have ancestors in any of four particular migrations of people from the British Isles to America, you'll enjoy David Hackett Fischer's *Albion's Seed: Four British Folkways in America*. He thoroughly describes four waves of English-speaking immigrants who came to America between 1629 and 1775. The first were the Puritans from the east of England to Massachusetts Bay. The second were the Royalist elite and their indentured servants from the south of England to Virginia. The third was that of the Quakers or Society of Friends who came to the Delaware Valley. And the fourth was the flight from the borderlands of northern Britain and northern Ireland who came to the American backcountry. This fourth group is called the Scots-Irish on this side of the Atlantic. These four groups of people brought their own customs, folkways, attitudes, rituals, traditions and ways of life.

This list of books could go on and on. Discussion of these mentioned is just to give you an idea of the kinds of books available that will help you understand your ancestors. Full citations for the examples are listed in the Resources section (Appendix B).

Famous Relatives

If you have an ancestor who was famous or associated with a famous person, read more about them. One researcher mentioned her family legend that her ancestor had been a body slave to Robert E. Lee, the Confederate general. She read several biographies of General Lee to learn about his farm, his lifestyle and his slaves. Her ancestor wasn't mentioned by name in the books, but she knows from her reading what her ancestor's life must have been like.

The famous person in your family may have been a collateral ancestor, someone related to you but not someone you're descended from. Investigate! Remember that family stories have a way of becoming distorted through the years. You may not be descended from Andrew Jackson (he didn't have children of his own), but if that story has been handed down in your family, look to see if you're related to the extensive Donaldson clan, the family of Jackson's wife. Or find out if you descended from another of Jackson's relations. A story has an origin somewhere, so don't discard it out-of-hand when it doesn't seem true upon your initial examination.

Remember, too, that everyone (well, nearly everyone) wants to have a connection to famous or heroic historical figures. Or infamous people. Hundreds of families throughout the Midwest have a family legend that goes something like this: "One night Jesse James came to the house with his band of outlaws. Grandpa let them sleep in his barn and they gave him a gold piece they stole in their last train robbery." Maybe an outlaw did sleep in Grandpa's barn, and *maybe* it was Jesse James. Read about outlaws in post-Civil War Missouri. Read a biography of Jesse James.

War and Other Momentous Events

Some of the momentous events in the nation's history have involved our participation in wars. You may be a Vietnam War veteran. Your father or uncles (or you, yourself) may have served in Korea or World War II. Your grandfather may have served in World War I. And his grandfather may have served in the Civil War.

As suggested, a time line is a way to pinpoint your ancestors who were of an age to have served in American wars. Once you identify the wars in which your ancestors might have been involved, you can search for military records. In the meantime, read about those wars. Review the listings under "Military Records" in the Resources section. For the recent wars, you may have information about your family member's participation.

Think about your ancestors' lives and what happened during the time they were alive. Who were the people in your family who might have been excited about the news of the discovery of gold in California in 1849? Did the stock market crash of 1929 have an impact on your family? What happened to your ancestors during the Great Depression? Did the great flood of the Mississippi River in 1927 affect your family?

Besides specific events, there are some topics of interest to genealogists in general and those deal with the facts of our ancestors' lives. Marriages,

DRAWING A TIME LINE TO FIND SOLDIER ANCESTORS

Who were your ancestors who might have served in America's wars? Right off, it may be a bit difficult to correlate dates of events with your ancestors' lives. Sometimes your brain needs a little help organizing information. If you create a diagram, it may help you see things a bit differently. Try the following technique and see if it works for you. If it helps clarify your thinking about your potential-soldier ancestors, apply it to other subjects.

Remember in school when you had to make a time line for a history assignment? Let's try it again. Tape some sheets of paper together, end to end, and draw a heavy line horizontally down the middle of them. Use a ruler and establish a scale. You might make one inch equal five years. Label the right end of the heavy line "the present." Mark the line off in increments and label them to suit your scale. Mark the decades on the heavy line—1990, 1980, 1970, and so on, backward in time for a couple of centuries. Then, above the heavy line, label the major U.S. wars on your time line, working back to the Revolutionary War.

War or Conflict	Dates
Vietnam	1954–1975
Korea	1950–1953
World War II	1939–1945
World War I	1914–1918
Spanish-American War	1898–1899
Civil War	1861–1865
Mexican War	1846–1848
War of 1812	1812–1815
Revolutionary War	1776–1783

Underneath the heavy line and parallel to it, draw another line representing your life. Begin the line at the year of your birth and draw it parallel to the heavy line on which you marked the dates. Drop down just a bit and do the same for your father's life span. If he's living, extend the line to the present, starting it at his birth year. Do the same for your grandfathers. And for your four great-grandfathers. Consult the family group sheets and pedigree chart you've compiled. You may not know the exact birth and death dates of all these men, so make an educated guess if you must, for now. Leave off your ancestors who never came to America. You'll have to consider their participation in wars in their native countries.

You've been drawing parallel lines so far, the heavy one representing the continuum of time and others representing the years of your male ancestor's lives. (We're just doing the guys in this exercise because soldiers were primarily male, especially in historic times.) Now use a highlighter or marker and draw a sweep of color vertically through the heavy line where you've marked off the war time periods, on through your ancestors' lines. Your object is to highlight the time periods in their lives when the wars occurred. Now compute their ages at the time of the wars from your heavy line. Some will have been children or older men during wartime. Any of the men who fall within possible military age on your time line may have served in the military.

Military age is relative. Henry N. Walls, my father, was born in 1901. He was too young to be required to register for the draft before World War I. His older brother got to go, but Henry didn't. He tried to enlist, but the recruitment officer knew the family and told him his mother's signature would be required. Henry's widowed mother had no intention of allowing her youngest to volunteer, so he missed out on the war. When World War II came along in 1941, he was past forty, too old to be drafted. But he enlisted anyway in the U.S. Navy's Seabees, a construction battalion. His father, James Henry Walls, nearly missed the Civil War. Born in 1846, he didn't turn eighteen until 1864. The war was still on when he became eligible, so he enlisted and spent the last year of the war in service. Allow a little latitude in your estimate of "military age."

Drawing the time line allows you to see the information about your family in a different way. You can use this technique for other historical events and include your female ancestors as well.

divorces, deaths, funerals and inheritance are topics that have been widely written about by social historians.

Marriage Records

When you looked for a marriage record in a courthouse, did you just look for your family members? Just the ones with the surname you're interested in? More experienced genealogists also pull out the records for collateral relatives, those descendants of long-forgotten aunts and uncles, brothers and sisters of their ancestor.

You can do more. Study that set of records. Look up the minister's credentials. In order to perform marriage ceremonies, ministers and other religious leaders had to bring evidence to the county clerk's office of their position in their religious body. Those credentials had to be transcribed into the county record books by the clerk. Those credentials usually identify the church or religious group that had conferred the status of minister. The records of that group may contain helpful genealogical information.

When you study that volume of marriage records, look at what's happening. If ages are recorded in that time and place, what is the average age at which women and men were marrying? Is your ancestor older or younger than average? Look at the age difference between brides and grooms—is the age difference different for your ancestral couple? Are there many marriages for senior citizens? What's going on in the community represented by those records?

Backing up ever further from the records, do some reading about marriage customs. David Freeman Hawke's *Everyday Life in Early America* briefly describes marriage customs. In Virginia, for example, he says a Southern wedding was a festive affair, followed by card playing, dancing, "an elegant supper" and singing. In New England, however, the Congregationalists had a different view. They saw it as a civil affair, officiated by a magistrate. Do some reading and learn about the customs involved in courtship and marriage for the time and place where your ancestors lived.

Divorce

You may encounter a divorce in your family. Don't let anyone tell you how rare it used to be. People in previous years divorced for many of the same reasons people file divorces today. Divorce rates did vary by region; they were lower in the South and higher in the West. And they were probably lower among some religious groups whose tenets especially forbade divorce. But they did happen. And they left records that often give a great amount of insight into family life.

To learn more about the subject of divorce, read Glenda Riley's *Divorce: An American Tradition*. Some of the information she relates about divorce laws is important when you begin a search of the records. Suppose, for example, a man disappears from the records, leaving a wife and children behind. You can't find a death record, no settlement of his estate, no divorce in the local records—just a missing husband. There's nothing in the records that actually says the woman is a widow, but you want to explain the disappearance. The information in Riley's book brings up an interesting possibility. The missing man may have left for the frontier—moved out west in search of gold, adventure, new possibilities. After fulfilling a short residency requirement in his new home, he could have obtained a divorce on grounds of desertion—hers, not his. Thus the records would be in some faraway place. But without reading about the topic of divorce, you might not consider all the possibilities.

Death Ways

One of the great preoccupations of genealogists is finding death records. You want those ancestors to live again by re-creating their lives, and you want to know when they died. It's often helpful to learn about the customs involved in funerals and burial to help you decide what kinds of records might be available to supply death dates. Reading books and articles about social history can help.

Look for sources about the time and place where your ancestors lived. If they lived in the Southern uplands you might read James K. Crissman's *Death and Dying in Central Appalachia: Changing Attitudes and Practices*. In it, he describes how mountain people felt about commercial funerals. They buried their own dead, with the neighbors helping to prepare the body for burial, until well into the mid-twentieth century. Predictably then, there was high noncompliance with the laws requiring death registration. Reading can give you clues to cemetery locations. In the upland South, Crissman quotes an older settler as saying graveyards were always located on high ground, never in valleys.

Your selection of reading material on this subject will be dictated by where your ancestors lived. When you visit a large library or use an online catalog, search under keywords for terms such as "funeral rites and ceremonies." Then look for material on your region and time period of interest.

A more general book on funeral homes and burial customs is *The History of American Funeral Directing*, by Robert W. Habenstein and William M. Lamers. It's not new, published in 1955, and probably only available in libraries and used bookstores, but it's filled with details about funeral customs and corpse preservation. If you wonder what the funeral ceremony was like for an ancestor who died in Victorian times, books like this one can supply minute details.

We're concerned with where our ancestors are buried, so cemeteries are an interesting subject for genealogists. David Charles Sloane's *The Last Great Necessity: Cemeteries in American History* describes the kinds of cemeteries used in America from frontier graves to well-tended memorial parks. Today, when we walk through a cemetery, we don't think much about trends in markers or why the place was selected as a cemetery site, but learning the history behind those places can furnish information about your family. If the cemetery is a commercial enterprise, someone bought the plot where your family is buried; records should be available.

Historical society journals often contain articles about particular cemeteries, but they don't often contain complete inventories of the interments; those are left to genealogical periodicals. To locate a history of the cemetery you're interested in may require an afternoon of reading tables of contents in back issues of the historical society's publication.

Inheritance

You're interested in inheritance because the records involved often supply the links between generations. When people leave wills naming their children, it greatly simplifies your research task. A study by three historians, Carole Shammas, Marylynn Salmon and Michel Dahlin, can help you understand this subject. *Inheritance in America: From Colonial Times to the Present* was first published by Rutgers University Press in 1987. It was reprinted in 1997 by Frontier Press of Galveston, and should be available in most libraries.

Laws about inheritance changed over time, and they differed greatly from place to place in the United States. Reading about the laws can help you decide which records to look for and what they mean.

Learning about the legal system in general, not just as it pertains to inheritance, can be of great benefit to you. If you want to start with an overview on the topic, read Lawrence M. Friedman's *A History of American Law*.

Expanding Your Reading

So many books, so little time. It's difficult to choose a starting place, so start with some volume that will give you a broad overview, then narrow

your focus. Keep pursuing footnotes. Maintain that list of books and articles to pursue. The Resources section in this book contains more suggestions for the kinds of titles you might read and full citations for the titles mentioned in this book.

Sources for Books

Your local library (including its interlibrary loan department) is your best source for the books mentioned. But we're acquisitive people, aren't we? You'll probably want to own some of your favorite books. And you may find some books of continuing value to you, so you'll want the convenience of having them in your home library.

Here are some tips on sources for books. You can buy them new from bookstores, of course, but only so long as they're in print and available from the publisher. Your library has access to the *Books in Print* series published by the R.R. Bowker Co. You can use this resource to tell whether a book is currently available and the publishers' addresses.

You may not be able to find (or afford) new copies of the books you're interested in. Used bookstores are wonderful sources for out-of-print and bargain books. Nothing beats going in person and spending an afternoon in a used bookstore. Visit the ones in your local area. Then there's Sam Weller's in Salt Lake City, Powell's in Portland, Half-price Books in Dallas (and elsewhere), and Shorey's in Seattle. But these and other good bookstores like them may not be within driving distance. With the Internet, more and more used bookstores are posting lists of their stock. And there are sites that link the used bookstores and let you search all their inventories at once with title, author and keyword searches. One of the largest online bookstores for new books is Amazon.com. More details about book sources are listed under "Vendors" in the Resources section of this book.

Libraries often hold used book sales. Join the Friends group for your library so you won't miss any sale announcements. Also, watch for notices about antiquarian book shows in your area. When the term "used" turns to "antiquarian," the prices go up, but the selection gets more interesting.

Build your personal library of historical titles as a sideline to your genealogy. But, whether you choose to borrow or buy books, continue to read about history to increase your understanding of your ancestors' lives and the events that surrounded them.

STEP 8

TAKING NAMES
Finding Census Records

Remember when the last federal census was taken? The government made a huge publicity effort to let everyone know how important it was to participate. The questions they asked weren't the same as in previous census years. Local government officials argued their areas were underreported. Finally, the numbers were in and it all blew over.

This description could have been written after any of the federal censuses since 1790, when the first one counted the inhabitants of the United States. In the name of equal representation, the Constitution mandated census-taking every ten years.

Census records are like a snapshot of the entire nation. The information gathered varied from census to census, but essentially, the process gives us a look at where everyone in the United States was as of a particular day. Or it was supposed to, anyway. The records accumulated by the census-taking haven't all survived. There were flaws in the system, but taken as a whole, federal census records are one of the most helpful bodies of records genealogists can use.

If you were to survey experienced genealogists on the topic of which single group of records is the *most* helpful for family history research, census records would top the list. They're a mainstay of genealogical research, and merit lengthy discussion here.

I will discuss the information available in each census year's records, and you'll see census records used in a case study on the Cates family. As you read about them, think of your family and apply the same research methodology when you're ready to venture into census records. You'll learn how to focus on your family's records.

First, a little background about the agencies responsible for creating the records may be helpful. The Constitution's directive that a census should be taken didn't offer specifics about who should do the job. From 1790 through 1840, federal marshals did it. They weren't necessarily the best-qualified people for the job, nor were they offered much training. They didn't even get preprinted forms until 1830. Pay was low and the job was tough.

For the 1850 census, a Census Bureau office was established in Washington, DC. The focus of census entries shifted from the family to the individual. Instead of devoting one line to a family, listing only the head of that family, the census in 1850 listed every person on a separate line in the returns. The Census Bureau was a temporary agency, resurrected every ten years to tend to the counting.

It wasn't until 1902 that a permanent Bureau of the Census was created as part of the Department of the Interior, then transferred to the Department of Commerce.

The Census of 1790

The 1790 federal census lists the names of the heads of households. People within each family were divided into the following categories: free white males of 16 years and upwards, free white males under 16 years, free white females, all other free persons, and slaves. The census was started on August 2, 1790, but it took until March 1792, to finish the job.

Native Americans weren't included in the census unless they were living as part of Anglo-American communities. If they were living with their tribal groups, they were considered "Indians not taxed," and weren't counted. The "all other free persons" category referred to persons considered "free people of color," that is, people who obviously weren't white, but were not enslaved.

The assistant marshals who did the enumeration were directed to copy their returns and post the copies in two public places in their assigned areas, so people could check them for errors. Then they forwarded them to the President.

Only about two-thirds of the 1790 census records survived. Those that exist were transcribed, indexed and published by the Bureau of the Census in 1908 as *Heads of Families at the First Census of the United States Taken in the Year 1790*, a 12-volume set available in many libraries. The original records themselves are available as a National Archives microfilm publication. For some states where the records are missing, tax lists have been published as substitutes.

The Census of 1800

The official date of the 1800 census was August 4. Beginning with the 1800 census, the federal marshals reported to the Secretary of State, instead of directly to the President.

In 1800, the marshals counted people in a more detailed breakdown by age than had been done in 1790. They counted free white males and females in age categories of 0 to 10, 10 to 16, 16 to 26, 26 to 45, and 45 and older. They counted the number of other free persons, the number of slaves, and they listed the town or district and county of residence. Most of the schedules were reported in the order in which they were enumerated, giving genealogists information about the people who lived near their ancestors.

The Census of 1810

In 1810, the census was started on August 6. The 1810 census was much like that of 1800. In this enumeration, marshals inquired about manufacturing establishments.

The Census of 1820

The official starting date for the 1820 census was August 7. For the first time, the marshals received printed instructions about how to conduct the census.

The reporting age categories were the same as the previous census, except for the addition of a category for free white males ages 16 to 18. The new nation, having just come through a second war with Britain, needed to know what its potential military strength was. The men counted in this category were supposed to also be included in the broader category of white males "of 16 and under 26," but there was some confusion about this among those conducting the census.

This census also counted the number of persons not naturalized (noncitizens), giving researchers some hints about when a family had immigrated to the United States. The number of people engaged in agriculture, commerce and manufacture were counted.

In this census, the manufacturers' schedules, separate from the population schedules, listed the owner's name, location of the business, number of employees, type of equipment, amount of capital invested, articles manufactured, annual production figures and remarks about the business.

The Census of 1830

The date of the census for 1830 changed from a traditional August date to June 1. For genealogists, that means there aren't ten full years between the census of 1820 and that of 1830. Thus a person born in June or July of 1820, who fell in the 0 to 10 age category in that census, might still be counted as under 10 years old as of June 1, 1830. The situation applies to some other age categories as well. The window of probability for this affecting one of your ancestors is small, but exists, nevertheless.

The June 1st date became the official census date through the 1900 census. For the census of 1830, the marshals were furnished with printed, blank forms to record answers for the first time.

The age categories for free white males and free white females were further broken down: 0 to 5, 5 to 10, 10 to 15, 15 to 20, 20 to 30, 30 to 40, 40 to 50, 50 to 60, 60 to 70, 70 to 80, 80 to 90, 90 to 100, and over 100 years. Age categories for free colored males and free colored females were: under 10, 10 to 23, 24 to 35, 36 to 54, 55 to 99, and over 100 years. Male slaves and female slaves were broken down in the same age categories as free colored persons. The 1830 census was the first to include a column with the total number of persons in the household.

The question about "foreigners not naturalized" was asked. And questions were asked about the numbers of "deaf, dumb and blind" persons in each household.

The Census of 1840

The census age categories remained the same as those of 1830. In this census, however, for the first time, the names and ages of Revolutionary War pensioners were provided. The questions about occupations were expanded to include mining; agriculture; commerce; manufacturing and trade; navigation of the ocean; navigation of canals, lakes and rivers; and "learned professions" and engineers. Questions were asked about the number of people in school and the number in the family who were over age 21 and could not read and write. The marshals also asked about the number of "insane" people, and they were supposed to distinguish between those in private care and those in public charge.

The Census of 1850

The census reports underwent a tremendous change in 1850. Every person was enumerated on a separate line in the returns, not just one family per line. The model for this census was one done in Boston in 1845, and it's of tremendous benefit to genealogists. The following information is listed for each person: name; age at last birthday; sex; race; profession or occupation; value of real estate; place of birth; whether newlywed; if attended school within the year; if the person could not read and write; if the person was deaf, dumb, blind, insane or "idiotic"; and if the person was a convict or pauper.

Slaves were enumerated on separate schedules (Slave Schedules) in 1850 and 1860. The name of the slave owner is listed, but the given names of the slaves aren't. Instead, they're identified by age, color, sex, and whether they were deaf-mute, blind, insane or idiotic; and whether or not they were a fugitive from the state.

A note should be added here about some of the terms used in old records. We don't call hearing-impaired people with a speech impediment "deaf and dumb" anymore. We don't refer to mentally disabled people as "idiots." (Of course, we're going to reach a point where bald people are "combing-impaired" or "folically-challenged.") But some of the words in old records *are* offensive to some people. If we change the words or labels, however, we may change the meaning of the information, so we're forced to leave offensive terms like "colored" in place. Remind the people you share your information with that the words aren't yours. Be careful not to apply today's definitions to yesterday's words. "Insane" in 1850 may have been applied to someone who drank alcohol to excess or had a severe case of PMS.

Birthplaces listed in the 1850 census were the state, territory or country; nothing more specific is usually given. Sometimes an examination of the birthplaces of a list of children in a family will show a migration pattern. The family's oldest children may list North Carolina as their birthplace; their nearest siblings may show Tennessee; and the youngest members of the family may have been born in Missouri, the place of residence of the family. By looking at the ages of the children, you can compute the dates they moved from one state to another.

Relationships between the members of the household aren't stated in the 1850, 1860 or 1870 censuses. A man, woman and group of children may be a nuclear family, but that is only implied and needs additional proof. Dwelling and household numbers are listed in the census. Each separate dwelling house received a number and there may have been more than one individual family under that roof.

In 1850, the first mortality schedule was compiled. Census enumerators asked each family if anyone had died there within the twelve months prior to June 1st. If so, the deceased person was listed on a separate schedule. Information collected included the deceased's name, age, sex, color, whether widowed, place of birth, month of death, occupation or trade, cause of death and the number of days ill. Mortality schedules, while taken at the same time as the population schedules, have been separated from them through the years, and the records exist in a variety of places. Several indexes have been published to the existing mortality schedules and can be located when searching the records of a particular locality. Mortality schedules accompany the censuses of 1850, 1860, 1870 and 1880.

The Census of 1860

The census of 1860 is much like that of 1850, though there are a few differences. The post office address is at the top of each census page in 1860. In addition to the value of real estate, a separate column in 1860 lists the value of personal property.

The Census of 1870

The census of 1870 was a repeat of 1860 with a few minor changes. In the column asking if a couple had been married within the year prior to the taking of the census, the enumerator in 1870 was supposed to write the month of the marriage. If a person was born within the year, the month of birth was supposed to be written in. If the parent of a person listed was of foreign birth, that was supposed to be noted in the appropriate column. The question as to whether someone was a convict or pauper was dropped. Slave schedules, of course, were discontinued. "Color" designations were supposed to be recorded more precisely: white (W), black (B), Chinese (C), Indian (I), mulatto (M). "Indian" meant Native American, not someone from India.

The Census of 1880

In 1880, the census underwent another big change. From a genealogist's standpoint, things got even better. Most all the same questions from 1850, 1860 and 1870 returns were retained, but there were important additions. For the first time, the relationships of people to the head of each household were recorded. Enumeration districts were listed, and in urban areas, street and house numbers were given.

The birthplaces of each person's mother and father (state, territory or country) are listed. It's secondhand information, but usually leads you in the right direction. Marital status is listed for the first time. Questions about the value of real and personal property were dropped. The question from 1870 about whether the parents were of foreign birth wasn't needed since birthplaces of parents were now listed.

The Census of 1890

Unfortunately all but one percent of the population schedules of the 1890 federal census were destroyed in a fire near Washington, DC, in 1921.

About half of a special veteran's schedule did survive the fire. Starting in the middle of the reports for Kentucky and continuing alphabetically through the states, the records survive. Each entry lists the Union Civil War veteran's name, widow's name, his rank, company, regiment, dates of service, post office address, disability and remarks. Sometimes Confederate veterans were listed, too, though often their names have a single line drawn through them on the reports, leaving them still readable in most cases.

The Census of 1900

The population schedules for 1900 were even more detailed than those of previous years. Month and year of birth are listed for each person. In addition to marital status, the number of years married, total number of children born to a mother, and the number of those children who were living at the time of the census are listed. The year of immigration and number of years in the U.S. are shown for foreign-born people. Questions were asked about whether the family's home was on a farm, and whether the home or farm was owned (and, if so, whether or not it was mortgaged) or rented.

The Census of 1910

Since 1830, June 1 had been the official census date. In 1910, however, the date was changed to April 15. The 1910 census dropped the question about month and year of birth. It added, for foreign-born people, a question about their native language. This census also shows whether someone was a Civil War veteran or the widow of one.

The Census of 1920

The date of the 1920 census was set as January 1. Though much like the 1910 census, it dropped the questions about Union or Confederate military veterans, number of children and duration of marriage. It added questions about the year of naturalization, and the "mother" tongue of the person and both of his parents. It asked the year of arrival for nonnative-born people.

The Census of 1930 and Beyond

The government has promised census records will remain confidential for seventy-two years after they're taken. That means the release date for the 1930 census should be in 2002. Availability may run a little later because copies have to be made and distributed.

The 1930 census is much like 1920. Additional questions were asked about employment. The 1940 census was the first to employ sampling, an advanced statistical technique. Enumerators in 1940 asked even more questions than in 1930 about unemployment, internal migration and income. It was the first to include a census of housing. These questions came as the nation was recovering from the Great Depression.

Sampling, used in subsequent censuses, means that some respondents answered a longer, more detailed set of questions than other people. Someday, future researchers will be delighted to find their folks were among the "sampled" because more information will be available about them.

You probably remember answering the census questions in 1990. A long paper form was mailed to your house. Perhaps you were among the "sampled" and received an even longer paper form. Did you think of making a copy of that form before you sent it in? Remember to do that when the census for 2000 comes around. Put the copy in with your collection of personal papers so when your descendants start a search of home and family sources, they'll have a head start on census research about you, and they won't have to wait seventy-two years.

Problems With Census Records

There are some general problems with census records. Spelling is probably the primary problem, compounded by handwriting difficulties. Today, spelling is set in stone; there's usually only one correct spelling of some-one's name. That's because most of us are literate, and we've been told spelling counts. Well, in the old days, spelling *didn't* count. Not only did people change the spelling of their names, other folks did it for them, too. Census enumerators were no exception. Whatever they could misspell (or spell in an alternate form), they did. Badly. Hughes could be Hewes, Moffitt might be Mawfit, Canard could go as far afield as Kinniart. Same people, same names, different spelling.

Whether you're using an index or reading the census schedules themselves, you must train your eyes to look for *people*, not names. If you're in doubt about the spelling of a name you find in the records, pronounce it aloud. Start a misspelling collection of your ancestors' names.

Handwriting can give you some grief. When you're working with census records, take some time to study the handwriting in the segment of the schedules you're interested in. Look for familiar first names—Sarah, Elizabeth, Laura, William, Robert, John, etc.—and study the letter forms in those words you know. They'll help you with the letters in unfamiliar names. Capital letter forms are especially troublesome. Again, find words you know in the same handwriting and note how the letters are formed. L and S, F and T, I and J can be easily confused. Penmanship classes used to teach old letter forms that we don't use any more. The one that troubles beginning researchers the most seems to be the double "s." When two lower-case "s" letters were written together, the first might be written as a "long s." A "long s" looked like an "f" or a "p," but the loops were turned differently. "Jesse" comes out as "Jeppe" or "Jeffe," "Missouri" looks like "Mifsouri," "Ross" is rendered "Rofs" or "Rops."

Abbreviations can create confusion, too. "Wm." for William, "Jos." for Joseph, and "Jno." for John are just a few. To add to your troubles, that "m" in "Wm." or the "os" in "Jos." were sometimes raised a bit above the base line, with perhaps a little dash line underneath them. When you're copying information from the census reports and run into these little quirks, copy just what you find in the record. That "Jos." you transcribed as "Joseph" may actually have been "Jas." for James.

There are other problems with the census as well. You have no guarantee everyone told the absolute truth to the marshal who appeared at the door asking such questions as how many convicts, idiots and paupers were in the home. You don't know which family member answered the questions. (Imagine your teenager answering the census questions.) Ages listed may be estimates. Watch for ages that end in zero—40, 50, 60—they may represent someone's best guess instead of an exact age.

Census instructions in 1850 directed the marshals to personally inquire at every residence, "and not otherwise," which meant in previous years they'd probably used other methods. You can't be sure all the instructions were followed. The information in the schedules was supposed to be given as though the questions had been asked on the official date of the census. Often, the inquiry was done weeks or months afterward. Babies born after the official date were supposed to be omitted, and people who had died since the official date were supposed to be listed as though living. It must have been confusing to all involved.

One of the most distressing problems you'll encounter is missing census records. Some of the schedules didn't survive. All or parts of census records for a particular state may be missing. And even in the surviving records, faded handwriting or poor microfilming may render the pages illegible.

Census records are based on state and county boundaries. And they may not be today what they were yesterday. United States history is about acquisition of land. New territories and states were added. County boundaries changed as more people moved into a region. The best source for learning about boundary changes is William Thorndale and William Dollarhide's *Map Guide to the US Federal Censuses, 1790–1920*.

Locating Copies of Census Records

Population schedules of the federal censuses are in the custody of the National Archives. All have been microfilmed and made available through microfilm publications.

The microfilming process involves using an overhead camera to photograph copies of original records and record them on photographic film. A master negative is made first, then copies are produced from it. Copies can either be made on silver halide film which is expensive but has a longer archival life, or by a diazo process which isn't as permanent but makes better working copies. Copies of microfilm purchased from the National Archives are silver film. Many commercial vendors sell copies of National Archives film either on silver or diazo film.

A microfilm reader is necessary to read the reduced images on microfilm. It uses a system of lens and mirrors to project the image onto the screen of the reader so it's large enough to read. Microfilm readers are available at nearly all public libraries. Many genealogists buy their own microfilm reader to use at home. Used readers may be as inexpensive as fifty dollars, or new ones, depending upon features, can cost over a thousand dollars. Reader-printers, those that have a built-in copy machine, are even more expensive.

So you, as a genealogist, have to locate the rolls of microfilm you need and be able to view them on a microfilm reader.

How are you going to decide which roll of film you need? When the National Archives makes copies of a microfilmed series of records, they give the group of microfilm rolls a publication number. Within each publication, they number the rolls of film. To help researchers locate the right publication, then the right roll of film, the National Archives has published four catalogs of microfilmed census publications. One covers 1790 through 1890, and there are separate catalogs for 1900, 1910 and 1920.

A complete list of National Archives locations are found in the Resources section (Appendix B) of this book. The microfilm catalogs are also available online at the National Archives' Web site, http://www.nara.gov /genealogy/genindex.html.

To use census records, you must have an idea about the time period your ancestors lived in a particular place. When you questioned your living relatives, you asked about where the family lived and who the family members were. This information can lead you to the right census reports. A case study in this chapter of census research on the Cates family illustrates the way you might approach census research.

Let's suppose you're interested in Texas County, Missouri. The catalog for 1920 lists the publication number as "T625" for the 2,076 rolls of film on which the population schedules of the 1920 census are filmed. When you read the listings for Missouri, you find Texas County was filmed on roll 965.

Now you need to get that roll of film. You could buy the roll of film from the National Archives, but that procedure gets a bit expensive. It's like buying every book you think might be helpful to your research—prohibitively expensive after a while. On the other hand, if you had many family members in Texas County and want to study the film again and again, you might consider buying a less-expensive, diazo copy of the film from a commercial vendor.

In an ideal situation, you live near a library that has at least part of the National Archives 1920 census microfilm publication. Now you must consider libraries' collection development policies. If you live in Missouri, there's an excellent chance your local library will have census film for your home state. Many libraries acquire census microfilm for their state and the surrounding states, or for the states that contributed to migration into the area. They might, instead, buy census microfilm for the entire United States before a certain time period—1850, for example.

If you live in Michigan and need census film for Missouri, you may have a problem. Perhaps the library has census film for Missouri, but only for 1880 and before. You might talk with the person who takes care of interlibrary loan at your local library. If you can supply the exact title of the microfilm publication and roll number, depending upon the library's interlibrary loan policy, you may be able to borrow the microfilm you need. Those catalogs of census microfilm listed in the Resources section will help you with the specifics about title and roll number.

If your local public library isn't a source for the census microfilm you need, contact a local college or university library and ask about their holdings. Or check for census microfilm availability in a nearby city's library.

If you live near Washington, DC, visit the National Archives. Or if you're within driving distance of one of the regional branches of the National Archives, you're in luck, because each has all the census film for the entire United States. A list of those branches is included in the Resources section of this book.

There are several commercial vendors who offer microfilm rental programs and their holdings usually include census microfilm. They frequently advertise in genealogical magazines such as *Everton's Genealogical Helper* and *Heritage Quest*.

The Family History Library in Salt Lake City has census microfilm for the entire United States. In addition you can access that film for a small rental fee at a local Family History Center. The Family History Library system is described in "Step 6, Branching Out: Beginning Research in Libraries and Archives," pages 58-59.

Though you should start with the most recent census available, sometimes, for practical reasons, you can't. If your local library has the 1900 census film for Texas County, Missouri, and you have enough information to identify your family in that census year, you may want to begin with the most recent census microfilm available to you. Once you find your family in any census, it's tempting to scurry backward in time through census records. But, wait—you might miss some important information if you don't pursue all the census records. So go ahead and use whatever census film you can find, but make the extra effort to borrow copies of all the census films that apply to your families.

By the year 2002 when the 1930 census is released, you may be an accomplished researcher digging through Colonial records. Do take the time to find your family members in what will seem like a very recent, redundant source. You never know what information is there and how it can help you learn about your family.

In recent years, a new distribution method for census records has started. Images of the census pages themselves, taken from microfilm, have been stored and distributed on CD-ROM disks for computers. Now they're only available for selected states and census years, but in the future they'll probably be produced for more places and time periods. This method of distribution has some obvious advantages. Personal computers are much more widely available than microfilm readers. Printing an image of a census page digitized on a CD-ROM is much easier than from a microfilm reader-printer.

Census Indexes

When you get ready to pursue your ancestors in census film, you may know the county and even the township or other minor civil division where they lived. If so, you'll be able to read the census film, moving from family to family, and find your folks. The census is organized first by census year, then by state, thereunder by county, and within counties by enumeration districts for 1880 and more recently, and by other civil divisions before that. So if you know your folks lived in the northern part of Texas County, Missouri, your search is a manageable one.

But what if your family members lived in St. Louis in 1920? You'll spend several days reading all the census microfilm for an area that large. Or, suppose you only know your family was from Missouri, and you don't know the county? Then you need an index to the census.

Indexes take several forms. Some have been published in book form, others are available on CD-ROM; some are National Archives microfilm publications. The kind of index you use will depend on what's been produced for a particular census time and place, and it will also depend upon your having access to that index.

Indexes for various states through 1870 have been compiled and published in book form by commercial publishers and some genealogical societies. The most prolific of the commercial publishers was a company known primarily as Accelerated Indexing Systems (AIS). AIS indexes aren't perfect, but there are an enormous number of them out there. The databases from which the index books were compiled were licensed to Automated Archives, an early publisher of genealogical CD-ROMs. Flaws in the AIS indexes didn't change when the data came out in electronic format. Many other companies have produced indexes, some overlapping the AIS indexes already in print. Whenever possible, it's best to use more than one index to a census.

Most indexes for 1850 through 1870 contain only the names of heads of household, not the names of everyone listed in the census schedules. Sometimes they also list people who have different surnames than those of the heads of household but live at the same address. Before you use any census index, read the introduction to the volume carefully. If the index is on CD-ROM, the text of the introduction is reproduced in a text file on the CD. Read it to learn the criteria used by the indexer. Learn about the flaws in the census film itself. If part of the film was very light or illegible, the compiler of the material may warn you about it in the introduction. There are several sets of numbers on the original census pages; read the introduction to learn which set of numbers the index compiler used.

No index is perfect. When you don't find an entry in an index volume, it means only one thing: you didn't find the entry. It doesn't mean the entry wasn't in the volume—it may have been under an alternate spelling. That alternate spelling may have appeared on the original census film or the indexer may have misread it. The index entry may have been miskeyed—two transposed letters can send an entry to Never-never land—or the indexer may have missed an entry or a segment of entries.

When you say you didn't find a family in the 1850 Missouri census, you probably mean you didn't find them in the 1850 Missouri census *index*, because it would take a very long time to look at every roll of microfilm in the census publication itself.

Census indexes are wonderful, but recognize their limitations. One way to work around imperfect indexes is to look for groups of people instead of just one family. If you can look up several associated people in a census index and find part of them in one location, you can then go to the census film itself and search for the ones you didn't find in the index.

Statewide indexes are ideal and let you search a wide area, but many local societies and individuals have published census indexes or indexed transcriptions of their county's census schedules. These are usually done by someone familiar with the family names in the county and can be very valuable. You may find these when you do a search for published materials about a particular location. Census indexes have also been a popular subject for local genealogical and historical society periodicals. These can be found through the *PERiodical Source Index* (PERSI) described in "Step 6, Branching Out," pages 59-60.

Soundex Indexes

There's another category of indexes made available by the National Archives as microfilm publications. These indexes are called Soundex indexes. In the 1930s, under the federal government's program Works Projects Administration (WPA), unemployed white collar workers began indexing the 1880 federal census. The Social Security program had been introduced as part of President Franklin D. Roosevelt's New Deal. Under it, workers were eligible for benefits when they reached a certain age. But many of those folks were born before birth certificates were required by law. Many didn't have birth certificates even when they were required to be filed. How were these people going to prove their ages? Indexing the census returns seemed like a partial solution.

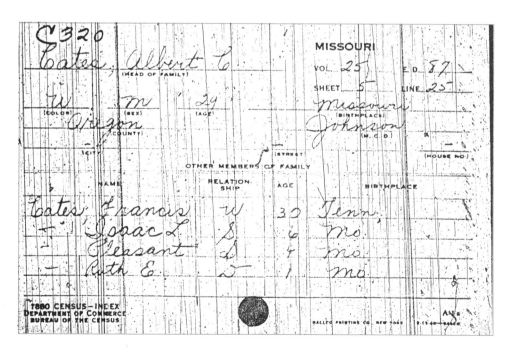

Figure 8-1. Soundex Card   This Soundex card has been reproduced from microfilm.

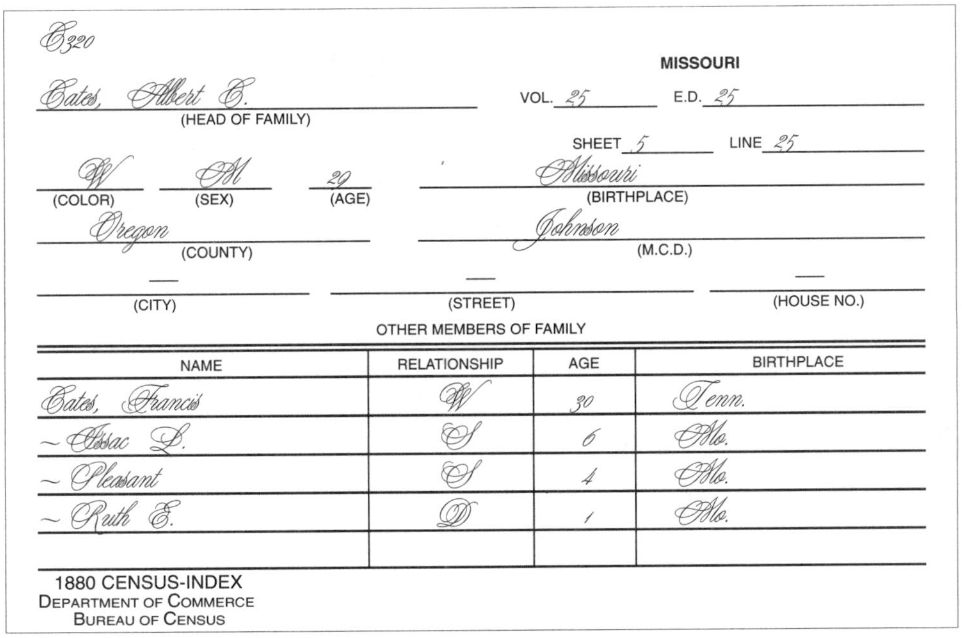
C320

MISSOURI

Cates, Albert C. VOL. 25 E.D. 25
(HEAD OF FAMILY)

SHEET 5 LINE 25

W (COLOR) M (SEX) 29 (AGE) Missouri (BIRTHPLACE)

Oregon (COUNTY) Johnson (M.C.D.)

— (CITY) — (STREET) — (HOUSE NO.)

OTHER MEMBERS OF FAMILY

NAME	RELATIONSHIP	AGE	BIRTHPLACE
Cates, Francis	W	30	Tenn.
~ Issac L.	S	6	Mo.
~ Pleasant	S	4	Mo.
~ Ruth E.	D	1	Mo.

1880 CENSUS-INDEX
DEPARTMENT OF COMMERCE
BUREAU OF CENSUS

Figure 8-2: Sample Soundex Card This is our re-creation of the Soundex card in figure 8-1. The Soundex code appears in the upper left corner. See the sidebar "Interpreting the Soundex Code" on page 96 for further discussion.

The WPA workers didn't index all of the people listed in the population schedules of the 1880 census. They only included families with children aged ten and under. They reasoned that older people listed in 1880 wouldn't be employed in occupations covered by Social Security. People who were out of their family groups for one reason or another, even though they were over age ten, are frequently included. Some of the index cards in the project seem to have been lost before they were filmed and occasionally cards were filed out of order. So the 1880 Soundex index isn't perfect, and it's a *partial* index to the households found in the census schedules.

The 1880 Soundex indexes are arranged by state, and thereunder by a numerical code which groups like-sounding names together. (See the sidebar "Interpreting the Soundex Code," page 96.) Within each code or group of codes, the cards are arranged in alphabetical order by the first name of the head of household.

WPA workers extracted family entries from the census schedules. They used index cards to record the information. The cards list the members of the households (those with children ten and under in 1880), their ages, race and birthplaces. The relationships among family members are shown. The county, minor civil division and citation to the census volume is listed, too. Sometimes the entries are continued onto a second and even a third card, if the family was large. In general, the handwriting on the cards is much better than that of the census schedules.

The same caution applies to this index as to any other—if you don't find the person you're looking for, it doesn't mean that person isn't listed in the census schedules themselves.

The 1900 Soundex index to the federal census schedules is much better than the one for 1880. First of all, it is an index to every family in the schedules (or it's supposed to be, anyway). A card was made for every head of household and entries on the card list all the people within that family. Cards were made for all adults at the same address but whose last names were different than the head of household. It seems to be more accurate than the one for 1880.

The 1900 Soundex index is arranged like the one for 1880. It's arranged first by state, thereunder by Soundex code number, and then in alphabetical order by the first name of the head of household. The scope of the 1900 Soundex is nationwide; it includes an index for every state and territory.

Just when things were looking up, the 1910 Soundex is a disappointment. First of all, it doesn't cover all the states, just the twenty-one states for which no vital records office existed at the time of the 1910 census: Alabama, Arkansas, California, Florida, Georgia, Illinois, Kansas, Kentucky, Louisiana, Michigan, Mississippi, Missouri, North Carolina, Ohio, Oklahoma, Pennsylvania, South Carolina, Tennessee, Texas, Virginia and West Virginia. (A wonderful Soundex index for Oregon's 1910 census has been created by members of the Genealogical Forum of Oregon.)

The 1910 Soundex and its close cousin, the Miracode index, were created by the Bureau of the Census. The coding system is the same for both, but the citations to the census schedules are a bit different. The Miracode indexes are machine-produced rather than handwritten. The accuracy of the 1910 Soundex and Miracode indexes is not good.

There are Soundex indexes for all the states in 1920, and while the accuracy doesn't equal that of 1900, it's much better than not having an index. Again, the heads of households and adults with different last names living in the same household are listed on the top of the index cards. Other people within the families are listed on the cards. Names in the index are grouped in numerical codes, then in alphabetical order by the first name of the head of household.

Remember, these Soundex cards are an index. Some researchers are tempted to copy the information from the Soundex card and skip the step of looking at the original census schedules. Don't be tempted. There is much more information in the census than just that on the Soundex cards, and you should read the names yourself to be sure the indexer copied them correctly.

The Soundex indexes produced by the WPA and the Bureau of the Census are National Archives microfilm publications. They're available through the same sources as federal census microfilm. And, like the census publications, they're listed in the census catalogs from the National Archives. (See the Resources section in this book.) Those microfilm catalogs are the key to locating the correct roll of film with the entries you need.

Microfilm of the Soundex indexes can be interlibrary loaned through participating libraries, rented through the LDS Family History Center network, or rented or borrowed through commercial vendors. Many large libraries have Soundex indexes to their census holdings for which those indexes exist. And they're available at the National Archives and all of its branches.

Soundex indexes aren't the only indexes available to the 1880, 1900, 1910 and 1920 censuses. As with earlier census schedules for particular counties, many genealogical societies and private individuals have published indexes or indexed transcriptions to their counties. Journals and periodicals have frequently published indexes to these censuses.

Other Census Finding Aids

Census indexes aren't the only tools that will tell you where your ancestors are in census records. Any document that shows where they lived can be a pointer to the census records. Deeds, rental agreements, mortgages, insurance policies, letters, diaries, voter registration cards, marriage licenses, newspaper clippings and a hundred other items can point you to a specific county. The closer you can come with one of these clues to a census year for which the records are available, the better your chances are of finding your folks. City directories can be especially helpful for locating your urban-dwelling ancestors in census records.

INTERPRETING THE SOUNDEX CODE

Soundex Coding Guide

The number		represents the letters:	
	1		B P F V
	2		C S K G J Q X Z
	3		D T
	4		L
	5		M N
	6		R

The letters A E I O U H W and Y are not coded.

The Soundex index is an index to the census records of 1880, 1900, 1910 and 1920. The index was recorded on index cards, and now is available through microfilm. The Soundex code (or the similar "Miracode" used in some 1910 records) is the mechanism for locating the census entries for your ancestors.

To locate an ancestor using Soundex, you must know (a) the state (or territory) in which your ancestor resided; (b) the census year you are searching; (c) the full name of your ancestor; (d) the approximate age of your ancestor; (e) the full name of the head of the household in which your ancestor lived (if at all possible.)

The Soundex is an index based on the way a surname sounds, so that a surname recorded under various spellings can still be located. To search for a particular surname, you must work out its code. The code will indicate where to start your search.

Every Soundex code consists of a letter, a hyphen and three numbers (e.g. *Brown* is B-650). The letter is always the first letter of the surname being coded and is not assigned a number. After the first letter, the letters A, E, I, O, U, H, W and Y are struck. The three numbers are assigned to the remaining consonants of the surname according to the following rules.

- Every Soundex code must be a letter followed by a three-digit number.
- A name with no consonants after the first letter, such as Lee, would be recorded with three zeros after the initial letter: L-000.
- A name with only one consonant after the initial letter, such as *Cook*, would be coded with two final zeros: C-200.
- A name with two consonants following the initial letter, such as *Smith*, would be given one final zero: S-530.
- No more than three digits are used; names with more than three consonants after the initial letter do not receive extra numbers. *Smithfield*, for instance, codes as S-531, and the additional consonants are disregarded.
- Double consonants, as in *Miller*, are coded as a single letter: M-460. The name *Lloyd* codes as L-300; the second *L* is not given a number because

L is the code letter for the name. *Scott* codes as S-300. The *S* and the *C* are considered to have an "equivalent value" because both C and G are coded with the number two, so the *C* is not coded. The two *T*s are coded as a single letter, and two zeros are added. A similar example is the name *McGee*. McGee is coded M-200 because the C and G are of "equivalent value" (both are coded as the number two) and are therefore coded as a single letter. Prefixes such as d', de, dela, de, du, le, van or von are sometimes disregarded in alphabetizing. Be sure to check for *Van Horn* under both V-565 and H-650.

Now try to code your own name:

_____ __ – __ __ __
_____ __ – __ __ __
_____ __ – __ __ __

Tips for using the Soundex

- The 1880 Soundex lists only those households containing children aged ten and under.
- The 1910 Soundex was done for the states of Alabama, Georgia, Louisiana, Missouri, South Carolina, Tennessee and Texas. The Miracode index was used for Arkansas, California, Illinois, Kansas, Kentucky, Michigan, Missouri, North Carolina, Ohio, Oklahoma, Virginia and West Virginia. All other states have no Soundex or Miracode records for 1910.
- The 1900 and 1920 censuses have a Soundex index for all states.
- Never stop researching with the Soundex entry. Always review the original census record.

State and Local Censuses

When we think about census records, it's *federal* records that come to mind first. All those records are available from one source, the National Archives. But those aren't the only census records that were produced. State and local governments also conducted censuses. Sometimes, those records are more difficult to learn about and locate, so they're not checked by beginning genealogists.

Information supplied in these state and local censuses varies considerably. Some were nothing more than a head count of the residents, and don't include people's names. Others are much more helpful.

For a complete list of state records, consult Ann S. Lainhart's *State Census Records*. For local census records, check the Locality Catalog for the area you're interested in at a local LDS Family History Center.

Clues in Census

When you find a census entry on one of your ancestral families, think of it as a starting place. Listen to the record, don't just read it. Here are some ideas:

In the 1910 census, if your ancestor (or his widow) is noted as having been a Civil War veteran, look for his name in Union and Confederate pension records (even if he died in the war and his widow applied for benefits). Then look for military records. Check for membership in organizations such as the United Confederate Veterans or the Grand Army of the Republic. Look for records of veterans' reunions. Often card files were kept of those attending those "good old boy" events. Check the 1890 veterans' schedules for information about your ancestor.

If anything points to land ownership, go to the deed books for the county of residence and search for purchases and sales of real estate. The 1900, 1910 and 1920 censuses ask if the residence is a farm or a home, and whether it's owned outright, mortgaged or rented. Value of real estate is one of the categories in the 1850, 1860 and 1870 censuses. Even if your ancestor was renting a farm, he may have mortgaged his tools or livestock to pay for other equipment, and that mortgage may be recorded in county records.

Value of personal property is listed in 1860 and 1870 reports. If your ancestors lived in a slave state in 1860, and if the value of their personal property is large, check tax lists, deeds, census slave schedules and probate records to learn whether they were slaveholders.

If the census shows someone in the family was a convict, look for prison records and court records. Check for newspaper accounts of the crime. Paupers in the family can lead you to poorhouse ledgers or county court minutes. "Idiots" and insane people may have commitment orders in the county court minutes and institutional records. Bizarre behavior also makes the news—if Cousin Albert was in the habit of wandering around naked in public (before his trip to the state insane asylum), it may have been a feature item in the local newspaper.

When the census indicates anything about marriage, it's time to look for marriage records. Census records for 1850, 1860, 1870 and 1880 ask if a couple was married "within the year," that is, during the twelve months prior to the taking of the census. 1880's reports even list the month of marriage. More recent censuses show the number of years married and often whether it was a second or third marriage for one of the parties.

Naturalization information can lead to citizenship applications and passenger arrival lists. Native-tongue data can lead you into foreign research.

Information requested about whether children had attended school within the year opens up the subject of school records. In addition, school news was often published in area newspapers.

Occupations listed in the census schedules should initiate questions about employment records and other business records. A blacksmith may have kept a ledger of his accounts. A minister may be written about in biographical publications specific to his church. Enumerators were directed to identify the denominations of ministers. Ministerial credentials may be on file at the county courthouse.

If any members of the families you find in census records lived to be remarkably old, there may be something in the newspaper about their deaths. The censuses from 1830 on identify the most senior of citizens.

Following clues in census records is a very broad subject—there are hundreds of possibilities. The point is to go beyond just reading the information about your family. Study it carefully and let it lead you to other records.

And don't just read the entries for your family members. Read about the neighbors. Were your folks more or less wealthy than their neighbors? Were they living in a neighborhood dominated by any particular ethnic groups? Were most of their neighbors literate? Read about the other people to develop a picture of the area. You're part of the neighborhood where you live; your ancestors were, too.

Many of these suggestions about following up on research suggest records found in courthouses, our next topic of discussion.

THE CATES: A TYPICAL CASE IN CENSUS RESEARCH

Jim wanted to know about his ancestors. He questioned his mother, Margie, about what she knew about her grandparents. She remembered her grandmother's name was Lula Mae Cates Teague and she was born in Many Springs, Missouri, on July 9, 1890. She'd visited her grave in Hickory Ridge, Arkansas, several times since her death in April 1958.

Margie remembered the names of her great-aunts and uncles as Julian, Henry, India and Cora. She wasn't sure about their birth order or their ages—just that they were Lula's brothers and sisters. Margie recalled a trip to Cotton Creek Cemetery in Oregon County, Missouri, to visit the graves of Lula's parents. She had noted the names and dates on the gravestones: Jefferson Davis Cates, 1861–1939, and Sarah Elizabeth Lucinda Robinson Cates, 1863–1939. Margie also remembered the names of Sarah Elizabeth's siblings as Will, Buddy (possibly his real name was Allen, she'd been told), and Martha, who'd married a man named Cypert. Margie had been told Sarah's mother, Mulbry Melinda, was half Indian and had come from Georgia.

Jim encouraged his mother to go through old family papers, and in an old box of her grandmother's photos, she found a list written by Lula's father, Jefferson Davis Cates, of the names and birth dates of his brothers and sisters:

Granville E. Cates, 9-10-1849
Albert C. Cates, 4-30-1851
Rosher Cursean Cates, 1-14-1853
Pleasant H. Cates, 2-12-1855
Mary E. Cates, 2-1-1858
Jefferson Davis Cates, 4-24-1861
Amanda Lusena Cates, 1-22-1864
Ephrain G. Cates, 5-5-1867

Jim copied the list into his notes but he didn't change the date format; he copied the dates just as they were on the list. And he made a note about his source and where he'd found it.

Jim decided his first step would be to order copies of the death certificates for Lula's parents. The certificates were very helpful. Sarah had died in May of 1939 at age 75 and her husband had followed in December of the same year. He was 78. The informant listed on both certificates was Julian Cates, one of their sons.

The death certificates gave Jim two new sets of grandparents. The parents of Jefferson Davis Cates were listed as Sack Lindsey Cates and Mulberry M. Williams. Julian didn't know where his father's parents were born. Jim immediately noticed that the information he'd gathered earlier was in conflict with that on the death certificates. Hadn't his mother said Mulberry (Mulbry in his notes) was *Sarah's* mother? Sarah's parents were listed as Andy Robinson, born in Illinois, and Sallie McGhee, born in Tennessee. Had Julian been mixed up about his grandparents, or was Jim's mother's information wrong? Jim had to reserve judgment on that point until he found another source.

Jim decided to try for a marriage record for Jefferson and Sarah. Since the birthplaces of both were listed as Oregon County, Missouri, he'd see if they were married there. He wrote to the Clerk of the Circuit Court and received the record, showing they were married December 17, 1879. Sarah's name on the record was "Elizabeth Roberson."

Jim decided he had enough information to venture into census records. He guessed the Cates were probably residents of Oregon County in 1920, but he didn't have access to the census film for that year. He decided to try 1910 and 1900. The library he visited only had the census film, not the statewide Soundex indexes. Rather than read all the names in the entire county, Jim located Many Springs on a map, the town he'd heard mentioned by his mother. It was located in the southeast part of the county, so he started his search in the townships of Johnson and Jobe.

In the 1910 census records, Jim found Jefferson and Sarah's children, Julian, Henry and India. They all three were grown and living in homes of their own. Julian, age 28, was married with a three-year-old son, and lived next door to Henry, age 26, also a married man with a four-year-old daughter and a two-year-old son. Both Julian and Henry had been married five years, and both of their wives were born in Kentucky.

Jim studied the neighbors listed in 1910. Just a few houses away were two families of McGehees, possible relatives. And next door to the McGehees was the family headed by Samuel Cypert, age 68, whose wife's name was Martha. Martha Cypert was 62, and Samuel was her second marriage. She'd been married to him for twenty-nine years, and was the mother of ten children, seven of whom were living. Her birthplace was listed as Tennessee. Was she the "Martha who married a Cypert"?

But where were Jefferson and Sarah? Jim expanded his search to include all of Oregon County, but they weren't listed. He knew from family information that Lula Mae hadn't married Arthur David Teague until 1911, so she and her younger sister, Cora, should have been listed in their parents' household. But where was it? Pressed again for information on this problem, Margie remembered her mother, Lula, had spent some time outside Oregon County one summer when they went to pick strawberries. The official starting date of the census in 1910 was April 15. Strawberries get ripe in May and are picked until mid-June. Possibly the family was gone at precisely the time the census was done. Jim checked the 1910 Soundex index for Arkansas but didn't find the Cates family.

Jim moved his census search to 1900. The Cateses were listed in Jobe Township, Oregon County:

J.D. Cates, born April 1861, age 39, born in Missouri, parents born in Tennessee

Lizzie Cates, born Aug. 1863, age 36, born in Missouri, father born in Illinois, mother in Ala. (they'd been married twenty years, and Lizzie was the mother of five, all living)

J.W. Cates, born Jan. 1882, age 18, born in Missouri

H.S. Cates, born Nov. 1883, age 16, born in Missouri

I.A. Cates, born Aug. 1887, age 12, born in Missouri

Lula Cates, born July 1890, age 9, born in Missouri

Cora Cates, born July 1894, age 5, born in Missouri

The Cateses' neighbors included the Cyperts, Robinsons and McGeehees. Jim noticed Jefferson's wife's name varied in different records. Her marriage license said "Elizabeth," this census showed "Lizzie," and her death certificate listed her as "Sarah E."

Jim's search turned up another Cates family in an adjoining township in Oregon County. The family of William C. Cates, age 34, born in Missouri, is listed. William's mother, Ava E. Cates, age 66, a widow, born in Tennessee, mother of eleven, with six living, was listed in his household. Since Jefferson didn't list a brother named William, and the name Ava was unfamiliar, Jim wondered who these "stray" Cateses were.

Jim decided to search for the Cateses in the 1880 census schedules. He expected to find them as newlyweds, based on their marriage date. He wasn't disappointed. J.D. Cates, age 19, and his wife, Sarah E., age 17, were living in Jobe Township, next door to a family of McGehees. Jefferson's birthplace in this record is listed as Arkansas.

In 1880, the returns for Johnson Township, Oregon County, list the following Cates families (see figure 8-4, page 104):

dwelling 38
Rozier C. Cates, age 27, born in Missouri, parents born in Tennessee
Mary A. Cates, his wife, age 20, born in Tennessee
Jefferson D. Cates, age 1, born in Missouri

dwelling 39
Sack L. Cates, age 57, born in Tennessee, parents born in North Carolina
Mulbury Cates, his wife, age 58, born in Tennessee, parents born in North Carolina
Ephrain Cates, age 13, born in Missouri
Martha Roberts, age 66, Sack's sister, born in North Carolina

dwelling 40
Albert C. Cates, age 29, born in Missouri
Francis Cates, his wife, age 30, born in Tennessee
Isaac L. Cates, age 6, born in Missouri
Pleasant Cates, age 4
Ruth E. Cates, age 1

dwelling 41
Pleasant H. Cates, age 25, born in Missouri
Melvina(?) Cates, his wife, age 17, born in Michigan

This census cleared up the discrepancy about whether the death certificate was correct about Jefferson Davis Cates's mother being Mulberry Melinda or the family information that Mulberry was Sarah's mother. She was surely Jefferson's mother. The list of siblings from the family records were nearly all present except Granville, Mary and Amanda. If married, the girls may have been right there, but Jim didn't know their new surnames.

Those "stray" Cateses from 1900 were listed in the 1880 census of Piney Township, Oregon County:

Ava E. Cates, age 46, born in Tennessee
Masqanck(?) Cates (female), age 17, born in Arkansas
William Cates, age 14, born in Arkansas
Parthenia Cates, age 11, born in Arkansas
Elizabeth Hill, age 76, born in Tennessee (Ava's mother)
Ephraim Cates, age 24, born in Missouri
Eliza Cates, (Ephraim's wife) age 22, born in Missouri
William Farris, (Ava's nephew) age 24, born in Missouri
Thomas L. Farris, (Ava's nephew) age 20, born in Missouri

Who were these people, Jim wondered?

In 1870, the "stray" Cates family is in Jobe Township, Oregon County (see figure 8-6, page 107):

Pinkney Cates, age 44, born in Tennessee

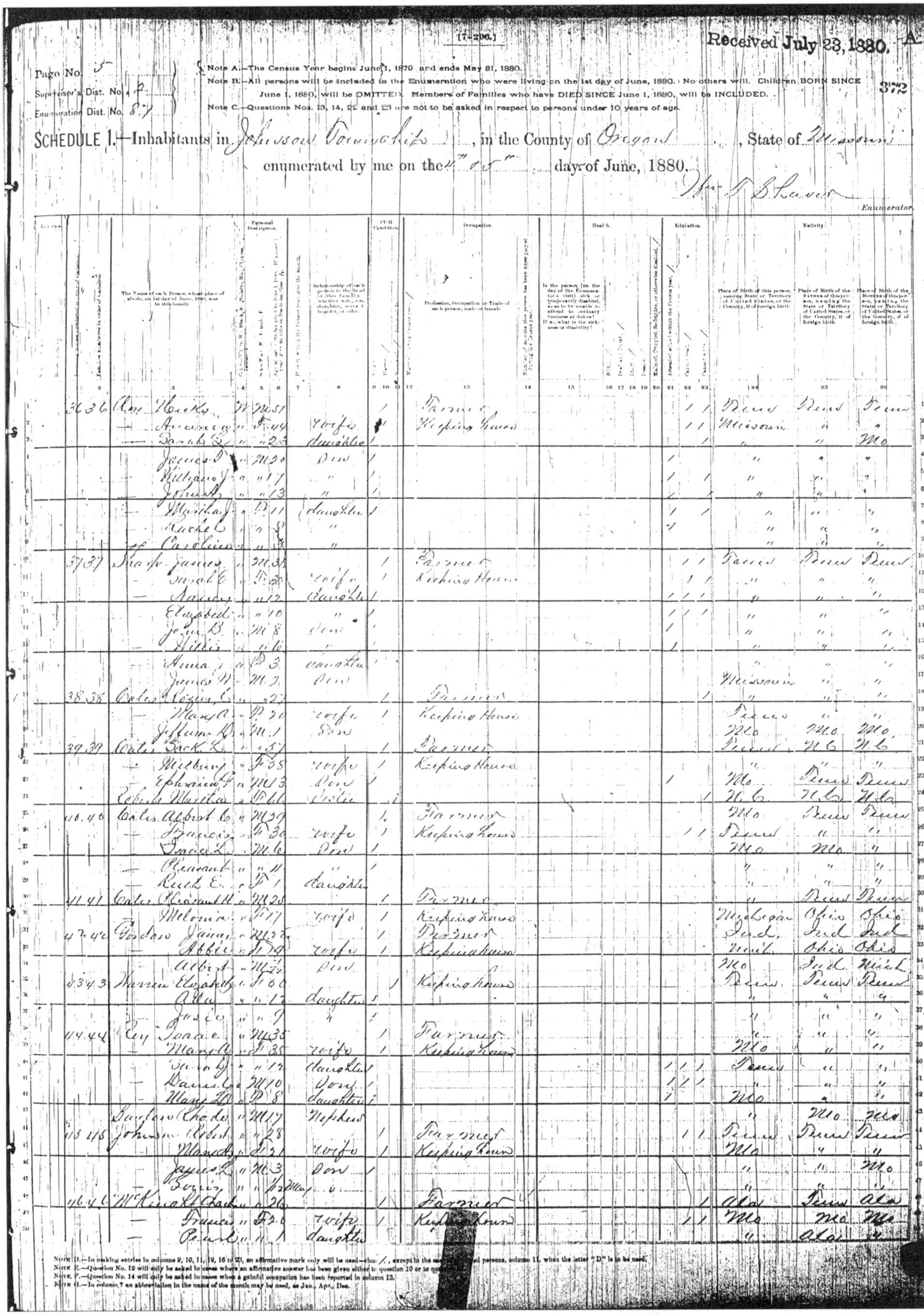

(7-296.) Received July 23, 1880. A

Page No. 5 | Supervisor's Dist. No. 4 | Enumeration Dist. No. 87

Note A.—The Census Year begins June 1, 1879 and ends May 31, 1880.
Note B.—All persons will be included in the Enumeration who were living on the 1st day of June, 1880. No others will. Children BORN SINCE June 1, 1880, will be OMITTED. Members of Families who have DIED SINCE June 1, 1880, will be INCLUDED.
Note C.—Questions Nos. 13, 14, 22 and 23 are not to be asked in respect to persons under 10 years of age.

372

SCHEDULE 1.—Inhabitants in Johnson Township, in the County of Oregon, State of Missouri, enumerated by me on the 4th & 5th day of June, 1880.

Wm T Shaver, Enumerator.

	Dwelling	Family	Name	Color	Sex	Age	Relationship	Occupation	Place of Birth	Father's Birth	Mother's Birth
1	36	36	Hicks, Am.	W	M	51		Farmer	Tenn	Tenn	Tenn
2			Amanda J	"	F	49	wife	Keeping House	Missouri	"	"
3			Sarah E	"	"	23	daughter		"	"	Mo
4			James P	"	M	20	Son		"	"	"
5			William J	"	"	17	"		"	"	"
6			John H	"	"	13	"		"	"	"
7			Martha J	"	F	11	daughter		"	"	"
8			Rachel	"	"	8	"		"	"	"
9			Caroline	"	"		"				
10	37	37	Sharp, James	"	M	38		Farmer	Tenn	Tenn	Tenn
11			Sarah C	"	F	30	wife	Keeping House	"	"	"
12			Nancy	"	"	12	daughter		"	"	"
13			Elizabeth	"	"	10	"		"	"	"
14			John B.	"	M	8	Son		"	"	"
15			Willis	"	"	6			"	"	"
16			Anna	"	F	3	daughter		"	"	"
17			James M.	"	M	2	Son		Missouri	"	"
18	38	38	Cates, Rozin C.	"	"	27		Farmer		"	"
19			Mary A.	"	F	20	wife	Keeping House	Tenn	"	"
20			Jefferson D.	"	M	1	Son		Mo	Mo	Mo
21	39	39	Cates, Jack L.	"	"	57		Farmer	Tenn	NC	NC
22			Milbury	"	F	58	wife	Keeping House	"	"	"
23			Ephraim G	"	M	13	Son		Mo	Tenn	Tenn
24			Roberts, Martha	"	F	66	Sister		NC	NC	NC
25	40	40	Cates, Albert C	"	M	39		Farmer	Mo	Tenn	Tenn
26			Frances	"	F	30	wife	Keeping House	Tenn	"	"
27			Isaac L.	"	M	6	Son		Mo	Mo	"
28			Pleasant	"	"	4	"		"	"	"
29			Ruth E.	"	F	1	daughter		"	"	"
30	41	41	Cates, Pleasant H	"	M	25		Farmer	"	Tenn	Tenn
31			Melonia	"	F	17	wife	Keeping House	Michigan	Ohio	Ohio
32	42	42	Gordon, James	"	M	2[illegible]		Farmer	Ind	Ind	Ind
33			Abbie	"	F	19	wife	Keeping house	Ind	Ohio	Ohio
34			Albert	"	M	[illegible]	Son		Mo	Ind	Mich
35	43	43	Warren, Elizabeth	"	F	60		Keeping house	Tenn	Tenn	Tenn
36			Ella	"	"	17	daughter		"	"	"
37			Josie	"	"	9	"		"	"	"
38	44	44	Coy, Isaac	"	M	35		Farmer	"	"	"
39			Mary A	"	F	35	wife	Keeping House	Mo	"	"
40			Sarah J	"	"	12	daughter		Tenn	"	"
41			Daniel C	"	M	10	Son		"	"	"
42			Mary D	"	F	8	daughter		Mo	"	"
43			Burton, Charles	"	M	17	Nephew		"	Mo	Mo
44	45	45	Johnson, Robert	"	"	28		Farmer	Tenn	Tenn	Tenn
45			Mandy	"	F	31	wife	Keeping House	Mo	"	"
46			James L.	"	M	3	Son		"	"	Mo
47			Rozin	"	"	1/12 May	"		"	"	"
48	46	46	McKnight, Charles	"	"	26		Farmer	Ala	Tenn	Ala
49			Frances	"	F	26	wife	Keeping House	Mo	Mo	Mo
50			Pearl	"	"	1	daughter		"	Ala	"

Note D.—In making entries in columns 9, 10, 11, 12, 16 to 23, an affirmative mark only will be used—thus /, except in the cases of married persons, column 11, when the letter "D" is to be used.
Note E.—Question No. 12 will only be asked in cases where an affirmative answer has been given either to question 10 or to question 11.
Note F.—Question No. 14 will only be asked in cases when a gainful occupation has been reported in column 13.
Note G.—In column 7 an abbreviation in the name of the month may be used, as Jan., Apr., Dec.

Figure 8-3: 1880 Census Page This 1880 census page was reproduced from microfilm. See figure 8-4 for a re-creation of the Cates entries.

Page No. ___5___

Supervisor's Dist. No. _2_

Enumeration Dist. No. _87_

Note A.—The Census Year begins June 1, 1879, and ends May 31, 1880. No others will. Children BORN SINCE June 1, 1880, will be OMITTED. Members of Families who have DIED SINCE June 1, 1880, will be INCLUDED.

Note B.—All persons will be included in the Enumeration who were living on the 1st day of June, 1880. No others will.

Note C.—Questions Nos. 13, 15, 22 and 23 are not to be asked in respect to persons under 10 years of age.

SCHEDULE 1.—Inhabitants in _Johnson Township_, in the County of _Oregon_, **State of** _Missouri_, enumerated by me on the _4th & 5th_ day of June, 1880.

Enumerator

Dwelling houses numbered in the order of visitation.	Families numbered in the order of visitation.	The name of each Person whose place of abode, on the 1st day of June, 1880, was in this family.	Color—White, W.; Black, B.; Mulatto, Mu.; Chinese, C.; Indian, I.	Sex—Male, M.; Female, F.	Age at last birthday prior to June 1, 1880. If under 1 year, give months in fractions, thus: 3/12.	If born within the Census year, give the month.	Relationship of each person to the head of this family—whether wife, son, daughter, servant, boarder, or other.	Civil Condition.			Place of Birth of this person, naming State or Territory of United States, or the Country, if of foreign birth.	Place of Birth of the FATHER of this person, naming the State or Territory of United States, or the Country, if of foreign birth.	Place of Birth of the MOTHER of this person, naming the State or Territory of United States, or the Country, if of foreign birth.
1	2	3	4	5	6	7	8	Single, / (9)	Married, / (10)	Widowed, /, Divorced, D. (11)	24	25	26
38	38	Bates, Rozier C.	W	M	47				/		Missouri	Tenn.	Tenn.
		—Mary A.	"	F	20		wife		/		Tenn.	"	"
		—Jefferson D.	"	M	1		son				Mo.	Mo.	Mo.
39	39	Bates, Jack E.	"	M	57				/		Tenn.	N.C.	N.C.
		—Mulberry	"	F	58		wife		/		"	"	"
		—Ephraim	"	M	13		son				Mo.	Tenn.	Tenn.
		Roberts, Martha	"	F	66		sister				N.C.	N.C.	N.C.
40	40	Bates, Albert C.	"	M	29						Mo.	Mo.	Tenn.
		—Francis J.	"	F	30		wife				Tenn.	Tenn.	Mo.
		—Isaac L.	"	M	6		son				Mo.	Mo.	Mo.
		—Pleasant	"	M	4		son				"	"	"
		—Rube E.	"	F	1		daughter				"	"	"
41	41	Bates, Pleasant H.	"	M	25						Tenn.	Tenn.	Tenn.
		—Melvina	"	F	17		wife				Michigan	Ohio	Ohio

Figure 8-4: 1880 Census These census entries were re-created from the 1880 census page shown in figure 8-3. The text of the form and of the entries is accurate.

Evaline Cates, age 36, born in
Tennessee
Thomas Cates, age 17, born in
Missouri
Ephraim Cates, age 15, born in
Missouri
Mary Cates, age 9, born in Missouri
Rebecka Cates, age 7, born in
Missouri
William Cates, age 4, born in Missouri
Parthenia Cates, age 1, born in
Missouri

At least we know who the missing father in 1880 was, though Ava's name was "Evaline" in 1870. The name so badly written for the female age 17 in 1880, is probably the Rebecka of 1870. Who were these people?

Jefferson Davis Cates's family wasn't anywhere to be found in 1870. But eight houses away from the "stray" Cates family in Oregon County was this family:

Andrew Robertson, age 34, born in
Tennessee
Sarah Robertson, age 36, born in
Alabama
Martha Robertson, age 13, born in
Missouri
Mary Robertson, age 10, born in
Missouri
Francis Robertson, age 8, born in
Missouri
Lucinda Robertson, age 7, born in
Missouri
Parlee Robertson, age 4, born in
Missouri
Andrew Robertson, age 2, born in
Missouri
Addie Robertson, age 1, month born
in Missouri

It was a good thing for Jim his mother remembered her grandmother's full name: Sarah Elizabeth Lucinda Robinson. He

might have dismissed the 1870 census entry showing Sarah as a child named Lucinda if he hadn't known about her full name. And so far, he'd found her last name as Robinson, Roberson and Robertson. Sarah's death certificate lists her mother's maiden name as "Sally McGhee." Sally is a nickname for Sarah, so it appeared Jim had located another generation of his ancestors on the census returns.

The Robertsons' next-door neighbors in 1870 were William and Martha Sypert and the family of one William McGhee, born in Alabama.

Jim didn't find Jefferson Davis Cates's family in 1870 when J.D. would have been a nine-year-old child. He knew what the family group should have looked like from his list and previous census information. They do appear in 1860, but not in Oregon County.

The 1860 census for Texas County, Ozark Township, Missouri, lists:

S.L. Cates, age 37, born in Tennessee
M. Cates, age 38, born in Tennessee
Alexander H. Cates, age 12, born in
Tennessee
Granville Cates, age 11, born in Illinois
Albert Cates, age 9, born in
Missouri
Rosier C. Cates, age 7, born in
Missouri
Ples. H. Cates, age 4, born in Missouri
Mary E. Cates, age 1, born in Missouri

Also in Texas County, but in Piney Township, are:

M.P. Cates, age 36, born in Tennessee
Avaline, age 37, born in Tennessee
Semantha, age 27, born in Illinois
F.M., age 9, born in Missouri
Thomas A., age 7, born in Missouri
Ephraim J., age 5, born in Missouri

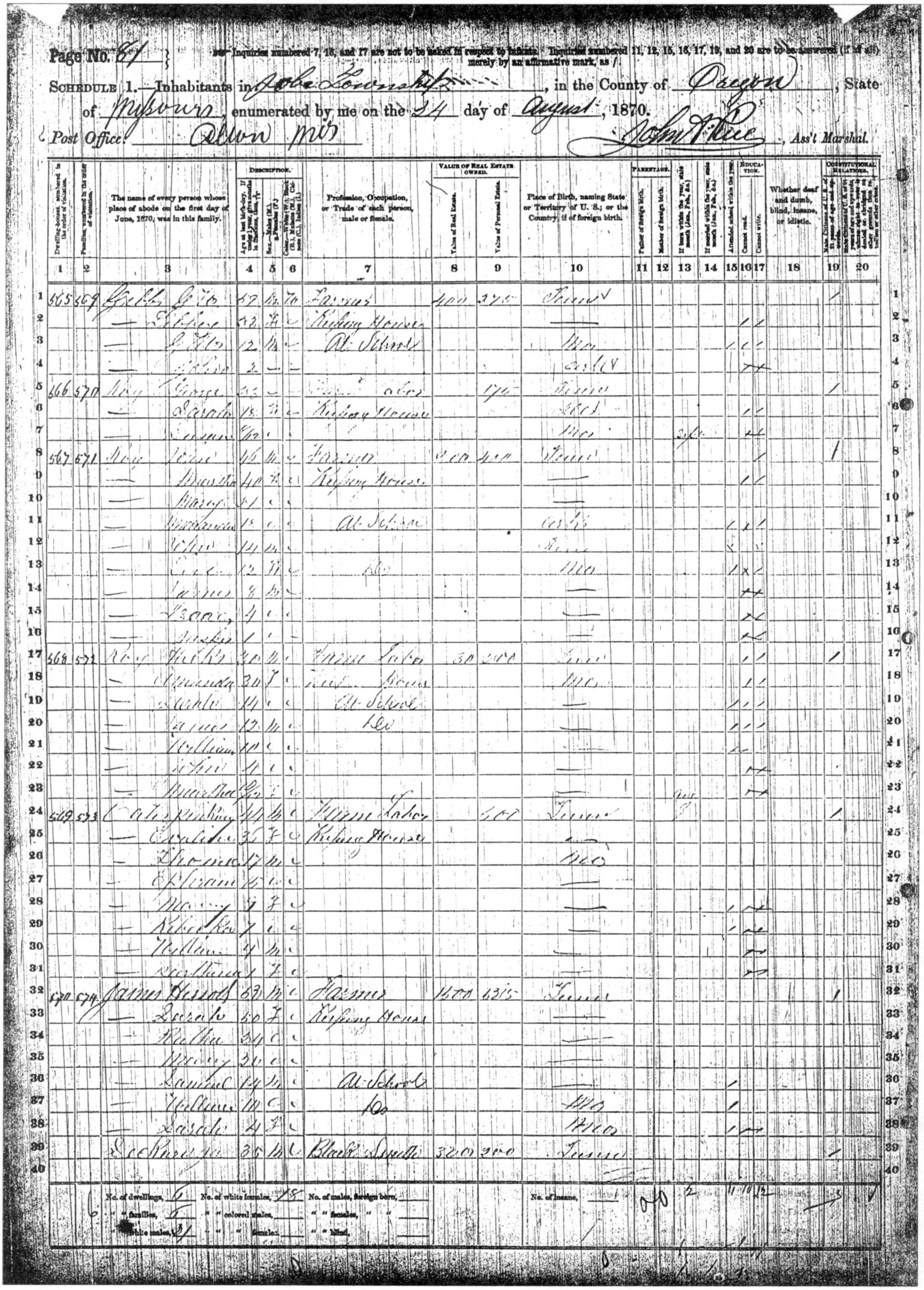

Figure 8-5. 1870 Census Page This 1870 census page was reproduced from microfilm. See figure 8-6 for a re-creation of the Cates entries.

Page No. _8_ } Inquiries 7, 16, and 17 are not to be asked in respect to infants. Inquiries 11, 12, 15, 16, 17, 19, and 20 are to be answered (if at all) merely by an affirmative mark, as /.

SCHEDULE 1.—Inhabitants in _Poke Township_, in the County of _Oregon_, State of _Missouri_, enumerated by me on the _24_ day of _August_, 1870.

Post Office _____, Ass't Marshal.

Dwelling houses (1)	Families (2)	Name (3)	Age (4)	Sex (5)	Color (6)	Profession (7)	Value Real Estate (8)	Value Personal Estate (9)	Place of Birth (10)	If born within year (13)	If married within year (14)	Attended school (15)	Cannot read (16)	Cannot write (17)	Deaf/dumb (18)	Male Citizens 21+ (19)	Male Citizens denied vote (20)
559	573	Bates, Pinkney	44	M	B	Farm Labor		600	Tenn.							/	
		~ Caroline	30	F	B	Keeping House											
		~ Thomas	7	M	B							/	/				
		~ Ephraim	5	M	B				Mo			/	/				
		~ Mary	9	F	B							/	/				
		~ Roberta	7	F	B								/				
		~ William	4	M	B												
		~ Parthenia	1	F	B												

Figure 8-6: 1870 Census These census entries were re-created from the 1870 census page shown in figure 8-5. The text of the form and of the entries is accurate.

("Semantha's" age is definitely listed as 27 on the census, so it has to be transcribed that way, but it's probably in error.)

The 1850 Missouri census index led Jim to Madison County, Missouri (see figure 8-8, page 110):

dwelling 528

Ephraim Cates, age 71, born in North Carolina

Rebeca Cates, age 56, born in North Carolina

Martha Cates, age 27, born in North Carolina

dwelling 529

Moses P. Cates, age 25, born in Tennessee

Evaline Cates, age 18, born in Tennessee

Semancy, age 1, born in Illinois

dwelling 649

Saml L. Cates, age 28, born in Tennessee

Melbina M. Cates, age, 28 born in Tennessee

Emaline Cates, age 5, born in Tennessee

Alexander M. Cates, age 3, born in Tennessee

Granville H. Cates, age 2, born in Illinois

Martha Cates, age 27, was undoubtedly the sister Martha Roberts, age 66, found in Sack L. Cates's home thirty years later. Since she's definitely Sack's sister and she's in the home of Ephraim Cates, there are strong indications Sack and Moses Pinkney Cates may be brothers. Relationships aren't stated among family members, so it would be dangerous to guess that Ephraim might have been the father of Sack and Moses P.—he's old enough to have been their grandfather, or he may have been their uncle.

The child "Semancy" in 1850 is probably one and the same as the "Semantha" in the 1860 census, though the age in 1860 is in error. Though Sack's name is spelled "Saml" in 1850, there's no doubt this is the correct family.

Drawing from the birthplaces of the children, it appears the families of both Moses P. Cates and Sack (Saml.) Cates were in Illinois in 1848 or 1849, and had only been there briefly before their move to Missouri. About 1847, the families had been in Tennessee.

But where are the Cateses in 1840? Probably in Tennessee, but only the heads of household are listed in the 1840 census. It's tempting for Jim to select *an* Ephraim Cates and decide he's the same Ephraim from Madison County, Missouri, in 1850. Jim knew he'd omitted county records. And he'd lost sight of the other people who were associated with the Cates family.

Starting in Oregon County, and moving backward in time to Texas and Madison Counties, Jim needs marriage, deed, tax and probate records for all the members of his family, not just his direct line. He needs to investigate all the records created during the time period his family lived in those places. He needs to pay attention to people like Mrs. Hill and the Farris nephews, peripheral folks who might provide clues to help with the Cates family. Then he needs to search for the whole group of people with whom the Cateses associated. They probably came from the same county in Tennessee. When he finds Ephraim Cates in Tennessee, he needs to be certain it's *his* Ephraim Cates and not a man by the same name. And all along the way, he needs to remember to record the sources for each piece of information so he can evaluate and analyze his findings.

	Dwelling-houses numbered in the order of visitation.	Families numbered in the order of visitation.	The Name of every Person whose usual place of abode on the first day of June, 1850, was in this family.	Age.	Sex.	White, black, or mulatto.	Profession, Occupation, or Trade of each Male Person over 15 years of age.	Value of Real Estate owned.	PLACE OF BIRTH. Naming the State, Territory, or Country.	Married within the year.	Attended School within the year.	Persons over 20 y'rs of age who cannot read and write.	Whether deaf and dumb, blind, insane, idiotic, pauper, or convict.
	1	2	3	4	5	6	7	8	9	10	11	12	13
1			Lycurder A Ashlock	21	m				Tennessee		1		
2			Mary A Ashlock	16	F				Missouri		1		
3			Joseph F Ashlock	10	m				Missouri		1		
4			The Self	7	m				Missouri		1		
5	522	522	Louis S Ashlock	25	m				Tennessee				
6			Sirina Ashlock	19	F				Missouri				
7			Polyphus Ashlock	1	m				Missouri				
8	523	523	John H Miller	57	m		Farmer	$2000.00	Virginia				
9			John S H Miller	19	m				Missouri				
10			Wm J H Miller	13	m				Missouri		1		
11			Martha A Miller	11	F				Missouri		1		
12			James M Miller	9	m				Missouri				
13			Sophia F Miller	7	F				Missouri				
14			Julian A Miller	5	F				Missouri				
15			Helen M Miller	3	F				Missouri				
16			Laura M Miller	1	F				Missouri				
17	524	524	Geo W McDowel	50	m		Farmer	$5000	N Carolina				
18			Martha A McDowel	29	F				Massachusetts				
19			Jno W McDowel	1	m				Missouri				
20			Sarah J McDowel	16	F				Missouri		1		
21	525		Fayette M Pease	27	m		Farmer		Connecticut				
22			Susan A Pease	19	F				Kentucky				
23			Joseph Kelly	24	m		Farmer		Tennessee				
24			Sarah E Kelly	18	F				Missouri				
25			Sarah E Kelly	2	F				Missouri				
26			Mary J Kelly	6	F				Missouri				
27	526	526	John S Haynes	45	m		Farmer	$1000.00	Virginia		1		
28			Julia Haynes	20	F				Missouri		1		
29			Elviry Haynes	18	F			1	Missouri		1		
30			Matilda Haynes	16	F				Missouri		1		
31			James Haynes	14	m				Missouri		1		
32			Susan Haynes	11	F				Missouri				
33			Louisa Haynes		F				Missouri				
34	527	527	Geo Matlock		m		Farmer		Tennessee				
35			Elizabeth Matlock	21	F				N Carolina				
36			Carrie A Matlock	5	m				Missouri				
37			Lewis Matlock	2	m				Missouri				
38	528	528	Ephraim Cates	71	m		Farmer		N Carolina				
39			Rebeca Cates	56	F				N Carolina				
40			Martha Cates	27	F				N Carolina				
41	529	529	Moses P Cates	25	m		Farmer	$1000	Tennessee			1	
42			Evaline Cates	18	F				Tennessee				

Figure 8-7. 1850 Census Page This 1850 census page was reproduced from microfilm. See figure 8-8 for a re-creation of the Cates entries.

SCHEDULE 1.—Free inhabitants in _____, in the County of _____ Madison _____, State

of _____ Missouri _____ enumerated by me, on the __ 2 __ day of _____ Sept. _____, 1850.

Peter R. Poado

Ass't Marshal.

Dwelling houses, numbered in the order of visitation.	Families, numbered in the order of visitation.	The Name of every Person whose usual place of abode on the first day of June, 1850, was in this family.	Age.	Sex.	Color. White, black, or mulatto.	Profession, Occupation, or Trade of each Male Person over 15 years of age.	Value of Real Estate owned.	PLACE OF BIRTH, Naming the State, Territory, or Country.	Married within the year.	Attended school within the year.	Persons over 20 y'rs of age who cannot read & write.	Whether deaf and dumb, blind, insane, idiotic, pauper, or convict.
1	2	3	4	5	6	7	8	9	10	11	12	13
58	58	Ephraim Cates	71	M		Farmer		N. Carolina				
		Rebeca Cates	50	F				N. Carolina				
		Martha Cates	27	F				N. Carolina				
59	59	Absol. D. Cates	25	M		Farmer	$400	Tennessee				
		Evaline Cates	18	F				Tennessee				
		Semancy Cates	1	F				Illinois				
60	60	Saml. L. Cates	28	M				Tennessee				
		Melvina M. Cates	28	F				Tennessee				
		Emaline Cates	5	F				Tennessee				
		Alexander M. Cates	3	M				Tennessee				
		Granville H. Cates	2	M				Illinois				

Figure 8-8: 1850 Census These census entries were re-created from the 1850 census page shown in figure 8-7. The text of the form and of the entries is accurate.

STEP 9

YOUR DAYS IN COURT
Research at the Courthouse

The records your ancestors left behind from their day-to-day business transactions in local courthouses can be wonderfully helpful in piecing together your pedigree. When you begin to build pictures of your ancestors' lives, they become real people, not just names and dates on a pedigree chart. Deeds, wills, mortgages, marriages, probate records, court records, tax lists and more were left in courthouses by your ancestors.

The key to getting the most from county records is knowing *where* your family lived so you can discover where they went to transact their business. Remember, political boundaries change over time. Consult Everton Publisher's *Handy Book for Genealogists* and Thorndale and Dollarhide's *Map Guide to the US Federal Censuses, 1790–1920* for county formation information.

When settlement began in an area, residents may have traveled many miles to the county seat, the place where local records were kept and court was held. As more people moved into that place, the residents might have petitioned the state or territorial legislature for their own, nearby county seat. Legislators listened to requests for closer, more responsive county governments and created new counties, establishing new county boundaries. The records about establishment and adjustments of county lines are found in the session laws passed by state legislatures. Through the years, as settlement continued to grow, even more counties were formed. So your ancestors may have lived in one place, but the name of their county of residence may have changed during their lifetimes.

Changes in county names and boundaries can become confusing. When you locate your ancestors in a particular county, search for information about when that county was formed, the counties from which its territory was taken, and subsequent counties formed afterward. Records about your family might be in any of those jurisdictions.

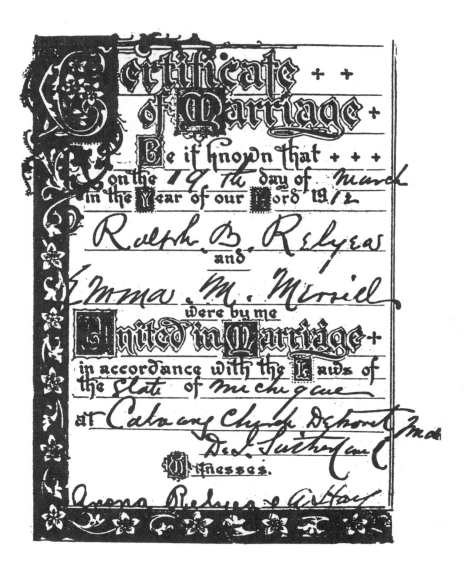

Figure 9-1: Relyea-Merrill Wedding Certificate This certificate, complete with the signatures of witnesses and the wedding party, is from a family Bible, probably the Bible given to the newlyweds as a wedding present. Unlike court records, however, this document is not acceptable as proof of marriage.

County seats changed, too. As counties were formed and divided, different towns may have been selected through the years as the place where the records were kept and court was held. In a pioneer area, the first seat of county government may have been a tavern or prominent person's residence. As the county began to grow, a building devoted to county business was constructed. That building, the courthouse, contained a meeting place where court sessions were held and an office for the county clerk. As the need grew, larger and more elaborate courthouses were built.

Courthouses were subject to disasters—fires, floods and tornadoes—

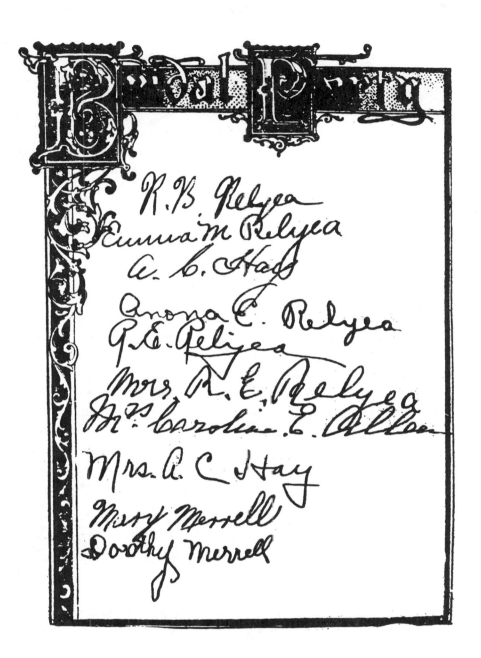

just like any other building. Sometimes the disaster was on a small scale; rodents, termites and other critters destroyed records, too. So even when you locate the right courthouse, the records you need may not have survived, but first let's talk about the kinds of records that might be available to help with your genealogical research.

While courthouses all over the United States have many elements in common, they also differ greatly. Clerks' offices are called by various names in different states. All courthouses don't contain the same kinds of records. So the information below about records is generalized. The best policy is to learn about the records for the county where your ancestors lived. Check Everton Publisher's *Handy Book for Genealogists* for information about a specific county's records.

Vital Records

When we think of vital records, those kept at the state level usually come to mind. But those records are often collected at the county level, and there may be copies of birth and death records in courthouses. State laws determine the collection and reporting procedures, so there are some states in which you'll find vital records at the courthouse and others where you won't. Some county-level recording of vital information predates state vital registration, and you may find those in the county records, too.

Marriage Records

In most states, marriage records are kept in the county records. Laws created differences in the kinds of information collected and recorded. And those laws changed through the years. Some marriage records are *just* records—the minister or justice of the peace who performed the ceremony stopped by the courthouse and reported the marriages he'd performed to the county clerk. In other times and places, a marriage license was required and the groom had to apply. Sometimes he needed a friend or relative to sign as bondsman, guaranteeing there were no impediments to the marriage and that it would take place.

Marriage records are usually kept in chronological order. When one rec-

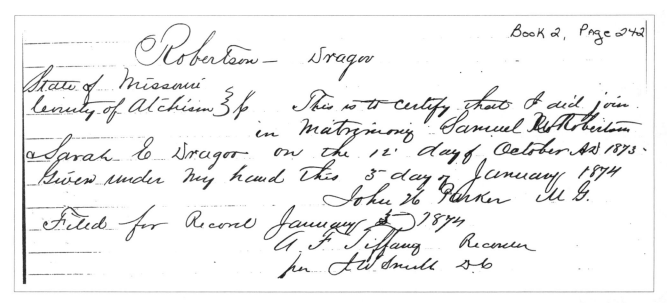

Figure 9-2: Robertson-Dragoo Marriage Return Although much more plain than the Relyea-Merrill certificate, this marriage return, copied from the marriage book at the courthouse in Atchison County, Missouri, constitutes legal proof of the marriage. Documents like this can often be ordered from the courthouse by mail or phone, or they may be available on microfilm through the Family History Library or the state archives.

ord volume is filled, another is started, and each covers a range of years. Each volume customarily contains an index. Sometimes the index lists both brides' and grooms' names, but frequently the index is only to the grooms' names. To find women when you don't know the names of their husbands, you must read through the marriage books themselves, scanning for brides' names.

Marriage records are usually found in the bride's county of residence, and that's the first place to search. But the couple may have been married in a nearby county, and the record will appear in that county's records. Or they may have traveled to the distant home of a relative for the ceremony. If you don't locate a marriage record or license, it doesn't mean your ancestors weren't married. Always check church records and newspaper articles for marriage information.

Probate Records

When a person died, the government, through the county courts, had an interest in seeing that person's property distributed to heirs, either according to the wishes of the deceased or in accordance with state law. If the deceased person left a will, a written document about who should inherit, it may be recorded in county records. Sometimes the will was written years before the death. When the person died, the executor, the person designated by the will to handle the estate, presented the will in court. Wills usually mention a person's children, giving genealogists links between generations.

If the deceased didn't leave a will (died intestate), the court appointed an administrator to oversee the estate. The administrator was often the spouse or child of the deceased. Usually they had to post an administrator's bond. Executors were required to post a bond, too, unless the wording of the will said otherwise.

The process of settling an estate created a number of records, depending upon the circumstances. If the deceased left minor children, a guardian was usually appointed to look after their interests. That person may have posted a bond to ensure any money or property was rightfully maintained. Sometimes an inventory was conducted of the deceased person's property. There may have been an estate sale, approved by the court, of the property of the deceased. Debts owed by the deceased had to be paid.

All of the paperwork involved in the settlement of an estate was usually bundled into a packet and assigned a case file number. Short summaries of the case's progress were recorded by the clerk in large bound volumes, called "minutes" books. Case numbers are sometimes written in the margins of the minutes books, or a separate index to the case file packets may have been maintained.

Probate cases are confusing to genealogists because the records are scattered in several sources. It's best to know what the law required for the

Application for Letters of Administration.

State of Missouri, } ss.
COUNTY OF ATCHISON.

In the Matter of *James A. Robertson* Estate.

Richard B. Robertson says that to the best of *his* knowledge and belief, the names of the heirs of the said *James A. Robertson* deceased, and their places and residences are respectively as follows: *Perry T. Robertson and Richard B. Robertson his Brothers; Martha Keer & Elizabeth Daily nieces and children of Jennette Daughter, dec'd,* who reside in the County of *Atchison* in the State of *Missouri; John Eli' Ida & Hattie Son* who resides in the County of *children of S. L. Smith deceased Sister Atchison,* in the State of *Missouri; Samuel H. Robertson a Brother* who resides in the County of *Cherokee,* in the State of *Kansas; Sarah Murry a Sister* who resides in the County of *Cherokee* in the State of *Kansas &c; Thomas W. Robertson a Brother* who resides in the County of _____; in the State of *Texas;* that the said *James C. Robertson* died without a will; that *Affiant* will make a perfect inventory of and faithfully administer all the estate of the deceased, and pay the debts as far as the assets will extend and the law direct, and account for and pay all assets which shall come to *his* possession or knowledge.

Richard B. Robertson

Subscribed and sworn to before me, this *17* day of *November* A. D. 18*74*

_____ Judge of Probate Court.

Recorded this *18"* day of *November* A. D. 18*74*

_____ Judge of Probate Court.

Figure 9-3: Application for Letters of Administration Probate documents like this one name heirs and the counties and states in which they live—fuel for further investigation! Probate documents may also reveal family friends and the married names of the female members of the family.

time and place of the death, then make a methodical search for all the pieces of the records.

A death doesn't always result in a probate record. If a person owned less than a certain dollar amount of property (which varied according to law) when he died, no estate settlement may have been required. And sometimes, even when a settlement was required, the family may have informally divided the property and never appeared in probate court. Occasionally, an estate settlement may appear as a deed in which the potential heirs are receiving their shares of the real estate. Women didn't have the rights they do today, and for most, there are no estate settlements separate from those of their husbands.

Some of the most informative probate cases are for childless people who owned property which had to be divided among siblings and nieces and nephews. So don't just look for records on people in your direct line—search for those collateral relatives, too.

Court Records

Court records can be helpful to genealogists. The probate court records discussed above are probably the most helpful court records, but records from other courts can be helpful, too. Court records can roughly be divided into civil and criminal records. Criminal court records often supply information that adds to your understanding of your ancestors. But civil actions have the most potential for family historians.

If an estate settlement in probate court didn't suit one or more of the heirs, they might have sued each other, or the executor or administrator, in civil court. Other disputes among people, including divorces, often resulted in court cases. Neighbors sued over boundary disputes and water rights.

When you begin a search for court records, it's helpful to know about the court system that was in place during the time your ancestors lived in the county. A small matter may have been tried in a justice of the peace court. A civil or criminal case may have been brought in circuit court. Some states maintained a separate equity court, called chancery court in some places, that contains a separate set of records to be searched. There are usually indexes to court cases, but sometimes the indexes don't list all the participants. It pays to look for the names of neighbors and relatives when searching court indexes.

Before 1906, naturalizations (the granting of citizenship to foreign-born people) were filed in most any court of record, including county-level courts. Those records may be found in courthouses. After 1906, naturalizations came exclusively under federal jurisdiction, and the records are found in federal court records. (See further discussion on page 120.)

Deed and Land Records

Records about land and property transactions can be exceptionally helpful to genealogists. Deeds are legal documents that transfer title in real property from one party to another. There are many different kinds of deeds, and reference works such as *Black's Law Dictionary* are helpful in learning more about deeds and other legal terms.

Usually the first acquisition of a parcel of land was from the government, either state or federal, and those documents conveying title are called grants or patents. They're often recorded in county deed books. Thereafter, sales are among individuals and those deeds are recorded in deed books.

The seller or grantor of a parcel of land wrote a deed conveying title to the buyer or grantee. The legal document was presented to the proper clerk of the county where the land was located and it was copied into record books. The original deed was given to the grantee, the new owner, for safekeeping.

Since ownership of land today involves proving chain of title, deed records, even the oldest ones, are considered "working" or active records in a courthouse. Title abstractors and attorneys use them daily, so they're accessible, not stored in an attic or basement of the courthouse.

Land records can be confusing, especially the legal descriptions of the property. There are two basic divisions of states in terms of land records: state-land states and public domain states. The state-land states are the thirteen original colonies and states created from them, plus Kentucky, Tennessee, Texas and Hawaii. The remaining thirty states are public domain states, so-called because their lands were once under the jurisdiction of the federal government.

All state-land states aren't alike in their land systems. The New England states used a "town system" in dividing parcels of land. Towns were the foundation of New England settlement, thus land records are found at three jurisdictional levels: town, county and state.

Southern and eastern state-land states use the "metes and bounds system," or indiscriminate survey system, where legal land descriptions are based on natural features and compass bearings, and aren't tied to any larger survey. This system was useful in well-settled European countries, but when transferred to the vast wilderness of America, it had shortcomings. In addition, natural features changed over time, leading to boundary disputes.

When the Revolution was over and Congress turned its attention to public lands, they authorized a survey system which divided the land into thirty-six-square-mile townships. In an area to be surveyed, a meridian line was run north and south. Baselines were established, running east and west. A grid of survey lines was imposed on the land so precise descriptions could be written. This is known as the Rectangular Survey System.

Knowledge of the survey system for the area where your ancestors lived is essential. Without it, the deeds you find will read like mumbo jumbo. Legal verbiage in deed records, and other records as well, can be confusing, too. A good legal dictionary will help.

Voter Rolls

Courthouses may contain lists of voters for elections held under the jurisdiction of county officials. Sometimes only current voter rolls are maintained, but old lists may exist in county records. Voter registration information may exist at city and state levels, too.

Voter rolls may seem to be of limited value, but some, depending upon time and place, contain physical descriptions, citizenship information and occupations, in addition to residence information. Recent voter lists may contain Social Security numbers.

Tax Lists

People have to pay for the government's operating expenses, and the records left behind in the tax collection process can be very helpful in your research. Just as tax codes today require some study to understand the rules, the old tax laws covered only some folks and certain kinds of taxable property.

The information in tax lists varies widely, depending upon time and place. In general, old tax lists contain the names of free adult males. Women are listed only in special circumstances. Sometimes a uniform head tax, or poll tax, was assessed on men of a certain age, whether or not they were property owners. Land, livestock and slaves were taxable property. In some areas, items such as gold jewelry and pleasure carriages were taxable items.

In order to use tax lists, you must learn what the laws required for the time and place where your ancestors lived. Then you need to know what records were created in the tax collection process, and, of those, which records survive. Once you locate the records, study their arrangement. Some are compiled in initial order, grouping all surnames together that start with the same letter. Others may be arranged by land description.

If you're fortunate enough to find ancestors living in a time and place where long runs of tax records are available, search through the tax books to learn more about your family members. Were they more or less wealthy than others in the area? Do you find the names of relatives, friends and fellow-travelers whom you know associated with your family?

When a new county was created, a copy of the current tax books for the annexed area may have been created. And even though a county's records may have been destroyed, check for tax book copies sent to state offices.

In many areas, substitute census records have been created from tax lists by genealogical compilers. They aren't as complete as a real census would have been, but they make excellent resources for genealogists. Remember to read the introduction to these secondary sources very carefully for information about what was (and was not) included.

Military Records

Military records for most American solders are held at the national level. The National Archives in Washington, DC, has records of soldiers from the Revolutionary War through the Spanish-American War (1898), including those for Confederate service in the Civil War. The National Archives branch in East Point, Georgia, has draft registration records for potential World War I soldiers. Records for soldiers in wars fought during the twentieth century are housed at the National Personnel Records Center in St. Louis (see Resources section, Appendix B).

America's soldiers were of two kinds: regulars and volunteers. Regular soldiers are what we think of today as career military servicepeople. Volunteer soldiers, even those who were drafted, are citizens called upon for service in times of war. The records for regular soldiers are filed separately from those of volunteers.

States often maintained records about their soldiers in an adjutant general's office or some other state-level agency. National and state records overlap in their scope. While most military records aren't local records, nevertheless, there are military records in local courthouses. Soldiers from World Wars I and II recorded their military discharges at their local courthouses. Depending upon time and place, militia lists sometimes exist in county records.

Besides military service records about the war experiences themselves, soldiers generated records as a result of applying for benefits. Most common were applications for pensions from the federal government. These came directly from Washington and little information about them exists in courthouses. Ex-Confederate soldiers applied for pensions from the state governments of Alabama, Arkansas, Florida, Georgia, Kentucky, Louisiana, Mississippi, Missouri, North Carolina, Oklahoma, South Carolina, Tennessee, Texas and Virginia. They applied according to their state of residence, not their state of service. While the pensions were administered at the state level, payments to veterans and their widows were often made through county offices, generating local records.

During the Civil War, some state governments passed laws directing county officials to care for indigent widows and children of servicemen. These "indigent lists" may be found in courthouses.

Soldiers who served in wars before the Civil War applied for bounty land under the various laws passed by Congress, and records about the land they received were generated at the county level when they recorded their land acquisitions.

Naturalization Records

Naturalization is the granting of citizenship to people from other countries. Because settlers were welcomed in the American colonies, naturalization consisted of little more than oaths of allegiance for people coming from non-British lands. When the United States was formed, Congress began to pass laws regulating naturalization. Since 1795, aliens have been subject to a five-year process for becoming citizens. In general, an initial application or "first papers" had to be filed, followed five years later by the filing of "final papers" in any court of record. In 1906, a major change took place in the naturalization process—naturalizations then had to be filed uniformly in federal courts.

Genealogists looking for naturalization records created before 1906 may find them in the papers of any court of record, including those in local courthouses.

Records Not in the Courthouse

There are records you won't find in the county courthouse where your ancestor went to do day-to-day business. The key to figuring out which rec-

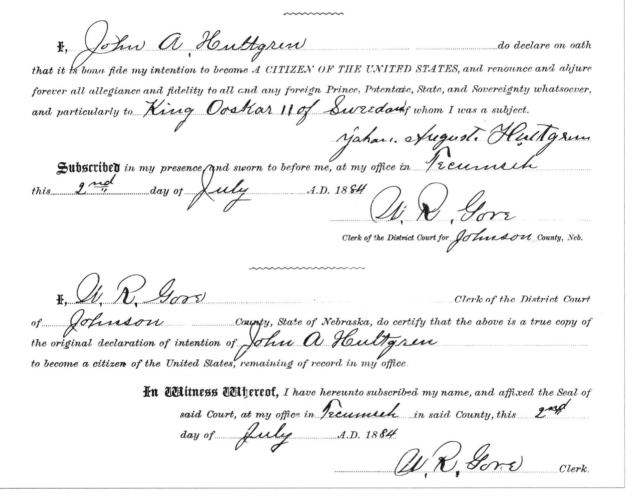

149.—DECLARATION OF INTENTION.

STATE JOURNAL Co., Publishers, Lincoln, Neb.

Declaration of Intention.

I, *John A. Hultgren* do declare on oath that it is bona fide my intention to become *A CITIZEN OF THE UNITED STATES*, and renounce and abjure forever all allegiance and fidelity to all and any foreign Prince, Potentate, State, and Sovereignty whatsoever, and particularly to *King Ooskar II of Swedan* of whom I was a subject.

Johan August Hultgren

Subscribed in my presence, and sworn to before me, at my office in *Tecumseh* this *2nd* day of *July* A.D. 18*84*

W. R. Gore

Clerk of the District Court for *Johnson* County, Neb.

I, *W. R. Gore* Clerk of the District Court of *Johnson* County, State of Nebraska, do certify that the above is a true copy of the original declaration of intention of *John A Hultgren* to become a citizen of the United States, remaining of record in my office.

In Witness Whereof, I have hereunto subscribed my name, and affixed the Seal of said Court, at my office in *Tecumseh* in said County, this *2nd* day of *July* A.D. 18*84*

W. R. Gore Clerk.

Figure 9-4: Declaration of Intention The declaration of intention was the first step in the naturalization process. This document was found in a family photo album and proved immensely valuable to the family genealogists. They were able to search the same courthouse for further information.

ords you won't find involves a magic word: *jurisdiction*. Public records are created because of legal requirements. The level of government involved determines where the records are kept.

Think about your own life. You're touching public records at different jurisdictional levels. When you get a parking ticket, you pay it at city hall, the municipal level. Your real estate taxes are paid at the county level; automobile tags are registered at the state level; and you pay federal income tax at the national level. Your ancestors' lives touched the records at these jurisdictional levels, too, though for different purposes.

Just as all the records about *you* aren't at your local courthouse, the records about your ancestors aren't either. If your ancestor's lawsuit against a neighbor was appealed to a higher court, the records may be in state jurisdiction. The land your ancestor acquired directly from the federal government has a land entry case file in Washington, DC, at the national level. Military records, as noted above, are usually federal records.

Private records are another category of materials you don't routinely find in courthouses. Newspapers, created by commercial publishers, are not public records. They do, however, contain information about courthouse business: news accounts of trials, land office notices, lists of delinquent taxpayers, estate settlement notices and other legal announcements. The best place to find newspapers is in libraries and archives.

Church records aren't public records, either. Ministers registered their credentials with the county clerks, and churches sometimes recorded their charters in county record books. Deeds for church property and cemeteries managed by churches are recorded in county deed books just like other land transactions. If some church matter resulted in a lawsuit, there will be public records about the case. But other than these kinds of matters, church records are private, not public records.

Before You Go to the Courthouse

Once you find the right county to search for records, your next step *isn't* to speed off to that courthouse. Of course, if it's nearby and convenient, do jump in your car and go. Chances are, however, the places your ancestors lived are far removed from your residence. The best way to start your research in county records is to visit a local Church of Jesus Christ of Latter-day Saints' (LDS) Family History Center. (The Mormons have a Web site with information about locations of Family History Centers. See "Step 6, Branching Out: Beginning Research in Libraries and Archives.")

Many county records of interest to genealogists have been microfilmed by the LDS Church. Marriages, wills, deeds, probate minutes, court records, and tax lists are available through Family History Centers. Using the records is a multistep process. First you must visit a Family History Center and use the Locality Catalog to find out which of the records are available for the county your ancestors lived in. The microfilm is housed in the Family History Library in Salt Lake City, and you can fill out rental requests and borrow the rolls you need.

It's much easier to use county records in air-conditioned comfort at a Family History Center than to poke around in a musty, dusty courthouse. Unfortunately, the Mormons couldn't microfilm everything. Some of the records you need may only be available by visiting a courthouse in person or hiring a researcher.

You may be able to write and request copies of specific records from the appropriate clerk's office, but don't expect courthouse employees to do research for you. Some county officials don't answer out-of-state requests at all. Others pass genealogy letters along to local people who do research for a fee.

Before you visit a county courthouse, do a little preparation. Write or call to be absolutely certain the records you need are available. Don't assume records created at the county level will still be at the courthouse—they may have been transferred to an archival facility. Or they may be stored in a warehouse and require an advance appointment so they can be retrieved. The courthouse may be closed for asbestos abatement or some obscure state holiday. On a not-so-obscure holiday, a researcher drove halfway across the state of Oklahoma only to learn Columbus Day was a holiday there, too. Local fair parades often close courthouses, and the days just before and after elections are a very bad time to visit.

Visiting a Courthouse

Anytime you do something new, you have to learn a few rules and a bit about how to conduct yourself. It's no different when you visit records repositories.

Remember your manners. Please and thank-you go a long way with nearly anyone, including courthouse staff. And they'll have more respect for you if they can tell you've done your homework in advance and know what you're looking for. Keep your requests brief and leave off the fascinating stories about your ancestors.

Wear business attire instead of your party-animal T-shirt and shorts. Yes, you're on vacation and perfectly within your rights to dress casually, but if you slip into a phone booth (well, maybe not a phone booth) and change into your Super-Researcher costume, you'll command a little more respect and attention from the staff. If you can't bear the thought of a tie or panty hose, pretend it's a costume party, and wear one or the other anyway. And leave your children, uninterested spouse and pets elsewhere.

Photocopies may be very expensive, and some of the record volumes you use may be too large or fragile to photocopy at all. Be prepared to take notes. Remember to use a research calendar and list all the sources you search, including the ones that weren't productive.

While you're searching, be sure to stay tuned in for the names of neighbors and associates of your ancestors. Notice who witnessed deeds and served as bondsmen for your family members. Make a note of the ministers who perform marriage ceremonies for your folks. In the record books, look well beyond the time you know your family lived in the area. Sometimes deeds weren't recorded until many years after they were actually signed. Estate settlements may not have been finalized until the youngest heir was of legal age. Don't just raid the records for names; study them carefully and listen to what they're telling you about your ancestors' lives.

Ask courthouse staff members for the names of local people who spend time poking around in their records. You may discover an expert who can help with your research.

Above all, remember to express your appreciation for the help you receive. A fruit basket or box of candy is appropriate for staff members who were especially kind and helpful.

Summary

Courthouse records can be wonderfully helpful to genealogists. Arm yourself with information about local history, knowledge of the structure of local records, and an understanding of the land survey system before you wade into the records. Think of yourself as a detective—courthouses hold the answers to many mysteries.

"JUSTIS OF THE PEAS"

Courthouse research is tough, but the payoffs can be extraordinary. Here's a true story in a fellow researcher's words that supplies some inspiration on this topic. The names have been changed— this could be your family line. The connecting clue you need could be in a dusty file in a courthouse.

"It didn't take me long to realize that no matter what name I chase, there are *at least* two men of the same name, and only one of them is mine. Bravely, I waded into the records of several William Freemans of New York state, one of whom had to be my ancestor who had migrated on to Michigan. Looking carefully at each, I began crossing them off my list of possibilities.

"It couldn't be the William in Westchester County—he was still on the census after my William had gone west. It wasn't the William in Broome County, because his census record listed only half the number of children

mine could boast. Not William in Saratoga County; I found a cemetery listing for him in a book at the library. I tossed out the W.T. in Oneida County and the William R. in Monroe County as well— they were simply the wrong ages. The William 'Treeman' who lived in Onondaga County was a tempting prospect because he did move to Michigan. I found a will for him with a bequest to a sister back in Onondaga County, but the names of his children mentioned in the will didn't match the names in my family.

"I was down to two men of the name—one in Cayuga County, the other in Genesee County. It was time for a courthouse trip. I marshaled my forces and put together everything I knew about my ancestor. I took information from his tombstone, the names and years of birth of his children from the census, and a copy of his will which named those children. I even studied his neighbors in Michigan with the idea that some of them might be long-time buddies who had lived near him back home. I hopped into my car and drove off in a fog of ancestral hopes.

"My first stop was the courthouse in Genesee County. There was nothing there to connect that William to my family. I was down to my last option, the William in Cayuga County. I was still green at the courthouse business, but I tried to follow all the rules. I arrived early in the day, nicely dressed, and I inquired politely, waited patiently for record books, and even refrained from telling the clerk my ancestor's life story.

"My efforts didn't appear to be working—it didn't seem to me the court minute books, deeds and tax lists were helping me decide if this was my particular William Freeman. In desperation, since it was now nearing the end of a long and fruitless day, I asked if there were other records I could see. I was trundled off to a dusty storeroom in the basement where I could examine the original case files of the county court.

"The court minutes mentioned a case in which a William Freeman was a witness, so I began to comb the storage boxes for a packet with that case number on the outside. The clock was racing. Fifteen minutes to five, and I finally found it. Folded up inside the packet were a number of small, irregularly shaped pieces of paper: a deposition from the plaintiff stating his view of the case, the judge's order releasing the disputed wagon to the victorious party, a yellowed newspaper clipping announcing the hearing in a legal notices column, and finally the report of a preliminary hearing in a justice of the peace court that had dissolved into a fist fight.

"What? I blinked, and blinked again. There at the bottom of that report was the signature of the official, 'Wm. Freeman, Justis of the Peas.' Loop for loop, letter for letter, the signature matched the one on the will in my file folder. I'd found *my* ancestor. I left the courthouse with a huge smile. That William Freeman of Cayuga County couldn't spell very well, but he was mine, all mine."

STEP 10

PUTTING IT ALL TOGETHER
Sharing Your Family History

You've tramped through countless cemeteries, talked to dozens of relatives, visited lots of courthouses, haunted scores of libraries and archives, and read countless books about history and research methodology. What's next? You didn't fill out all those family group sheets and enter all that computer data just for yourself, did you? It's time to share them with your nuclear family, extended family and distant genealogy cousins. After you've been through the genealogy learning process, it's time to share general information about what you've learned with others who are just starting their family history research.

Genealogy can be a great way to pull your family closer together. Involve your spouse and children and turn this pursuit into a family affair. Plan family vacations around your research needs. Surely there's a water theme park along the route to a courthouse you want to visit. Contact the Chamber of Commerce or tourism office for the areas you're interested in and ask about accommodations and attractions. One-half of the parent partnership can take the kids on a walking tour of the historic district while the other does research in the courthouse or library. Remember not to inflict your small children on the courthouse staff or librarian, but do take them to cemeteries and museums.

Use genealogy as a way to put your children in touch with grandparents, aunts and uncles, and cousins who live in far-away places. Encourage them to write letters and send E-mail messages to relatives. They can share drawings, photos and stories about day-to-day events.

Involving your children in the research process will not only give them a sense of their heritage and ancestors, it can sharpen investigative and reasoning skills they can use in other areas of their lives. Let them develop map-reading and geography skills as you share what you've learned about your ancestors.

Organizing a Family Reunion

Participating in a family reunion is a way to share your information with family members outside your nuclear family, and learn more at the same time. If your family holds an annual reunion, be sure to get involved. As you talk with distant members of the family, ask if they hold reunions. Make plans to attend. Many families schedule get-togethers on Memorial Day, Independence Day and Labor Day. For ideas on preparing a family reunion, look up *The Family Reunion Handbook*, by Thomas Ninkovich and Barbara E. Brown.

Family reunions can be small-scale affairs where all the brothers and sisters of a particular couple gather and bring their offspring for a big family meal. Or they can involve hundreds of people descended from a common ancestor of the Colonial period congregating from all over the country and spending a weekend at a resort.

If your family doesn't have an ongoing reunion, you can start one. First, call a meeting of your relatives who have expressed an interest in gathering the family together. You can meet in person or with a conference telephone call. Form a reunion committee. Pool your address books to make a list of all your relatives on that family line. The committee member who uses a computer can be appointed the list manager; the member who lives in the area where the reunion will be held can be the local arrangements manager; someone with creative ideas can be the entertainment manager. Your cousin with artistic talent can design announcement flyers. Other responsibilities can be meted out according to talents and interests.

Decide on a time and place for the event. Start planning early so vacation time can be reserved by those family members who are gainfully employed. Some employers require employees to choose vacation time around the first of the year. No date will suit everyone; there will always be people who have prior commitments.

Select a place for the event. An ancestral hometown or city convenient for many family members is a good choice. Look for a park pavilion, community meeting room or some other public meeting place that can be reserved in advance. Be sure to pick one with adequate space for the number of folks who'll attend. And no place will suit everyone, either. Do try to select one with hotel facilities in the area; it isn't fair to descend on one cousin's home.

Notify everyone on your mailing list about the reunion as soon as you have set the date and place. Ask them to respond to your announcement letter with the addresses of more cousins who might be interested. Plan to mail at least two flyers—one early and the other a few weeks before the reunion. Ask attendees for money to defray the cost of postage, phone calls and renting a site for the event. Suggest that each person make a small contribution. Keep track of the money—how much was received and where it went—in case someone asks. Advertise your reunion in area newspapers and genealogical publications.

Encourage everyone to bring their photograph albums to share with others. Plan special activities but leave unstructured time for visiting. Consider awarding inexpensive prizes or certificates for the oldest and youngest people in attendance, the person who traveled the longest distance to attend, the baldest, the tallest, the couple married the longest time, the most newlywed couple and other categories. You might conduct a search for the person at the reunion who most resembles a photo of great-grandfather. Line up the contestants, then have family members vote with their applause.

Encourage your reunion committee members to plan activities that will entertain and tie the family together. Organize tours of the local cemeteries where family members are buried. Make a wall-size display of the family tree and let people write their names on paper leaves and pin them on the tree. Be sure everyone at the reunion wears a name tag large enough to be read in photographs taken at the reunion. Appoint a camera person and reporter to videotape interviews with family members. Show the video of last year's reunion.

Plan ahead for the meals involved, and be sure the burden doesn't fall too heavily on one or two family members. Consider a potluck supper if most family members are within driving distance. If you're holding the reunion in a hotel's meeting room, talk with the banquet staff about setting up a special buffet for your group. When planning your meals, consider special dietary requirements for health and religious reasons.

Use the reunion event itself as a research laboratory—question family members about births, marriages and deaths in their branches. Ask about career and school accomplishments. Note new phone numbers and addresses. Record variations on family stories that have come down through other branches of the family.

Perhaps you can share the information you've already found in your research. Consider compiling a book about your findings. Start early on this project, it will take more time than you think.

Writing Your Family History

Whether at the family reunion or from other sources, you've probably gathered a large amount of information about your family lines. What are you going to do with it?

If you feel disorganized, go back and reread "Step 5, A Place for Everything: Keeping Records." Arranging your findings gives you another chance to analyze and evaluate what you've turned up.

Don't wait to "finish" your research—genealogy doesn't end (every ancestor has two parents); all you can do is choose convenient stopping places. Perhaps you've reached a point where you must make a research trip to find more information, but you can't leave career and family responsibilities to go. Maybe the records are available to you, but they just don't answer your questions about the links between the generations. Call a halt for the time being and write about your findings. Possibly a family reunion is coming up and you want to share your findings with your cousins. It's time to write.

If you've been entering data into a computer program, you can experiment with the report functions to print out your information in a variety of ways. But a genealogy is more than just a list of your ancestors; it's the *story* of those folks, too. Include legends and tales you've heard, and interesting tidbits you've turned up in your research. Write about problems you've encountered. If you can't identify an ancestor's parents, say so. And say why. Perhaps someone else will take up your work in coming years and solve the problem.

Arrange your information in some kind of logical order. Often the best choice is to pick an ancestral couple and write about them and their descendants. Patricia Law Hatcher's book, *Producing a Quality Family History*, can be of tremendous assistance. It tells you how to organize and arrange your findings and how to present them in a logical, well-structured order. Also useful is Kirk Polking's *Writing Family Histories and Memoirs*.

If you're using a computer program to manage your genealogy information, it will help you print out your findings. But don't be tempted to print out a series of family group sheets as a substitute for a correctly numbered family history. (You might, however, print family group sheets to take with you in a notebook to gather information at the family reunion.)

When you write about your family, stick to the facts. Let them speak for themselves. Don't be tempted to make up dialogue or interject what you think their motives might have been. Write about what you've found in the records, and what you think it means, and be sure your readers can tell the difference. Collect photos and documents and draw maps and diagrams to supplement your story.

Remember the previous admonitions in this book about writing source citations for every bit of evidence you gather? You'll need those citations now. When you write your family history, you want your family members to admire and respect your words. They'll do that more readily if you supply the information about *how* you know what you know.

Publishing Your Family History

Publication of your family history can be as simple as taking your camera-ready pages to a local photocopy shop and having several copies made. ("Camera-ready" means the printed pages will look just like the ones you've prepared on your computer or typewriter.) Add card-stock covers, choose a binding option, and you can have inexpensive books to share with your family members. If you need less than one hundred copies of your book, the photocopy method is probably the most economical choice.

For larger print runs you might consider commercial printers who specialize in family histories. These companies aren't *publishers*, they don't market or advertise your book. Be careful to investigate carefully before you select a printer. Beware of anyone who claims there are profits to be made on family histories; the profits they're referring to are *their* profits, made at *your* expense.

Prices per-book decrease as you increase the number of copies you have produced at one time by a commercial printer. The ideal number of books to have printed is enough so that you won't have to immediately reprint the book, but not so many that they sit unsold in your garage for years to come. Tom and Marilyn Ross discuss these topics in detail in *The Complete Guide to Self-Publishing*.

Distributing Copies of Your Family History

Some genealogists give away copies of their family history publications, but most people can't afford to do that on a large scale. Many family histories are sold for a price that covers printing costs and advertising fees, but genealogists rarely recover the cost of the research that went into the book's production. It's a labor of love, and even at that, it's difficult to sell family members a fifty-dollar book.

As a beginning genealogist, keep in mind that you'll probably want to share your research results at some time in the future. Gather the names and mailing addresses of everyone you talk with about your family—they're potential buyers of your book. Start a separate address book for your genealogy cousins. Be sure to note how they're related to you. Some genealogy computer programs offer an address-book feature to help you manage these contacts.

When you publish family material, send an announcement to everyone connected to the family line you've written about. This sale flyer or brochure should describe the book in detail, state the price and postage costs, and encourage purchase of the book. Some authors of genealogy books do this *before* they actually commission the printing, in order to determine the number of copies in the press run. This is called a *pre-publication sale* and the flyer and other promotional material should state very clearly the anticipated shipping date for the book. And that date should have a margin for delay built into it.

An Internet Home Page

There's another, less expensive, way to publish your family history. Set up an Internet home page. Commercial companies establish informational sites on the World Wide Web, and you can, too.

All of your family members can read the book you publish about your genealogy, but chances are, all of your relatives aren't computer users with an Internet connection. If you only display your family information on a Web site, you won't reach all your cousins. So an Internet site about your family can be a dynamic way to share your findings, but you may not want to make it the *only* way you distribute your information. Also, while Web pages have a useful role in the distribution of your data, they aren't permanent. If you want to ensure the family information you've compiled is around for a long time to come, do organize it into book form and distribute it as widely as possible.

How do you set up a family Web page? First, you need a computer equipped with a modem, a device that lets your computer speak to other computers over telephone lines. Then you need an Internet service provider who provides access to the amazing matrix of computers called the Internet. To learn more about this topic, read Cyndi Howells's book, *Netting Your Ancestors: Genealogical Research on the Internet.*

The monthly access fee you pay for Internet service often entitles you to a noncommercial Web page at no extra charge. You can learn how Web pages are constructed by reading a book or taking a class (it's really very simple), or you can let genealogical software programs simplify the task even more for you.

On a Web site, you can post tremendous amounts of genealogical data, scanned images of documents you've found, photos and lists of your cousins' addresses. You can add sound clips of voices or songs, and short segments of video.

One of the most exciting aspects of a family Web page, or any Web site for that matter, is that you can update as often as you want. When you discover a new set of grandparents, you can post the information quickly. You can add updated photos every week of your new grandbaby. It's a great way to advertise that family reunion, and you can maintain an up-to-the-minute list of the folks who've let you know they'll attend. The possibilities are endless.

Joining Genealogical Societies

So far we've talked about sharing your genealogy research results with your family members. Beginning genealogists think of family members as familiar faces. With more research, they discover distant cousins. Finally, they see the whole world as a giant network of related people. We're all cousins. Genealogists are those folks who know how we're all related.

And all of us like being among people who share our interests. Join a genealogical society in your area. It's fun being able to get excited about a death certificate among folks who understand. Enjoy the friendship of people who share your passion. Learn from others who've already cleared the research hurdles you're facing.

Most genealogical societies offer regular meetings and some kind of periodical. Some are entirely devoted to genealogy; others masquerade as historical societies. Some focus on a particular county, others are statewide in focus, still others are ethnic-group specific. Join a group in your local area, even if you have no roots there. Remember the adage, "what goes around, comes around"? It's true in genealogy, too. If you join your local group, even though you have no ties to the area, and help with records restoration projects and cemetery inventories, someone in the place where your ancestors lived will do the same.

Consider joining the local society where your ancestors lived, even though it's a long-distance membership. You probably can't attend the meetings, but you'll benefit from their periodical and they'll gain your financial support.

To find a group in your area, call your local library and ask for the name of a contact person with a genealogy or historical society. Or check newspapers' lists of upcoming meetings. After you've found the group, ask for membership information and sit in on a regular meeting or two. Visitors are always welcome. Watch for announcements about special genealogical workshops and seminars.

Continuing education departments of local schools and colleges often offer genealogy classes. Be a wise consumer—contact people who've taken a previous class from the same instructor and ask how they feel about their learning experience.

The kind of learning that can assist your genealogical endeavors isn't limited to genealogy workshops and classes. Sign up for a title abstracting course offered to real estate agents so you can learn how to read deeds. Take a course on surveying. Enroll in a nonfiction writing improvement class. Take a class on effective communication skills.

Much of the information about genealogy research methodology is available in the form of taped lectures on audio cassette tapes. Various genealogy organizations regularly hold conferences and seminars around the country. They invite experienced researchers to present lectures on a variety of topics. Those presentations are taped and sold by Repeat Performance, a company that specializes in capturing learning experiences on tapes. (See "Methodology Guides" in the Resources section, Appendix B.)

To learn about genealogical societies in distant areas, start with the membership directory for the Federation of Genealogical Societies (see the address under "Educational Experiences" in the Resources section). The Federation is an umbrella group for state and local historical and genealogical societies, family associations and libraries. Not every group belongs to the Federation, but it's a good starting place. Their membership directory lists contact information, officers names, periodical information, meeting dates and more. For Internet users, the Federation maintains a Web site with information about its group members.

Nationally distributed genealogy magazines such as *Heritage Quest* and *Everton's Genealogical Helper* periodically contain lists of state and local societies. The reference librarian at your local library has access to directories of organizations. Most societies have posted Web sites—use a search engine to find the Web address. Or you might just call a local library in the county where your ancestors were from and ask for details about the local genealogy group there.

Don't just join genealogy groups—participate in them. Get involved. Genealogy societies run on volunteer effort. Share your information. Share with family, near and far. Share with other researchers. And share yourself with genealogical and historical groups.

Bottom Line

You started this search for information because you wanted to know who *you* are. Follow the suggestions in this book and you'll learn about your ancestors, that marvelous group of people who contributed to your gene pool, who had an impact on who *you* are.

Genealogy is exciting! It's so personal—a journey of self-discovery. When you read court records about your great-grandfather's fits of temper, perhaps you'll better understand where those little tantrums come from in your close family members. When you feel an urge to pull up stakes and take a job in some distant state, you'll know your ancestors had itchy feet, too.

Don't keep this hobby to yourself. Encourage your friends, neighbors and relatives to search for their ancestors, too. We're all part of a global community. We're all cousins.

Appendix A

Guide for Source Citations

The purpose of this basic guide to source citations is to take the mystery out of writing information about how you know what you know. Don't worry about the commas and periods; they'll vary according to different guides anyway. But do read the examples to learn what you need to record about the material in which you find information about your ancestors.

The examples given are for footnote listings; bibliography entries will be different in their structure. If you have enough information to write a footnote for your family group sheet, you'll have enough to write the bibliography entry when you get around to compiling your family history.

When you begin to write a source citation, think about the readers who will come after you. Could they take the information you've supplied and easily find the material again? It's better to write too much about a source than too little.

Source	Footnote Example
Article	Morton Gitelman, "The First Chancery Court in Arkansas," *The Arkansas Historical Quarterly* 55 (Winter 1996): 357-382.
Bible Record (attempt to list provenance; that is, say who the Bible has belonged to in previous years)	Family data, Robert Harmon Williams Family Bible, *The Holy Bible Containing the Old and New Testaments* (New York, n.p., 1890); original owned in 1997 by Desmond Walls Allen. The Bible was passed from Robert H. Williams to his son, Curtis H. Williams, and by Curtis to his great-niece, Desmond.
Birth Certificate (state)	Hadley Edward Hirrill, birth certificate no. 103-81-001272 (1981), Arkansas Department of Health, Division of Vital Records, Little Rock.
Book	Jane Gray Buchanan, *Thomas Thompson and Ann Finney of Colonial Pennsylvania and North Carolina* (Oak Ridge, TN.: privately printed, 1987), 238-259.

Source	Footnote Example
CD-ROM	Heritage Quest, *Pennsylvania 1870 Census Index Entire State*, CD-ROM (Bountiful, UT: AGLL, Inc., 1997), John Smith household, Washington County, 210.
Cemetery Marker (secondary source)	Wanda M. Newberry Gray, *Cemeteries of Sebastian County, Arkansas,* vol. 1 (Fort Smith, Arkansas: privately published, 1997) 47 (Evans Cemetery).
Cemetery Marker	Harrison Williams tombstone, Herpel Cemetery, Stone County, Arkansas (5 miles E of Mountain View at Herpel); photographed by Thurlow Williams, 1988.
Census, Federal, 1790–1840 (microfilmed)	Maryann Hightower household, 1840 U.S. census, Izard County, Arkansas, page 196, line 15; National Archives microfilm publication M704, roll 18.
Census, Federal, 1850–1870 (microfilmed)	Nathan Moffitt household, 1850 U.S. census, Lawrence County, Arkansas, population schedule, Strawberry township, page 310, dwelling 428, family 437; National Archives microfilm publication M432, roll 27.
Census, Federal, 1880–1920 (microfilmed)	Jonathan Jones household, 1880 U.S. census, Faulkner County, Arkansas, population schedule, Cadron township, enumeration district 42, supervisor's district 1, sheet 12, dwelling 223, family 228, National Archives microfilm publication T9, roll 43.
Church Record	David Grimes admitted to membership, 2 October 1889, Record Book 2, 1888-1893: page 27, St. James Methodist Church, Stone County, Arkansas; Hendrix College Library, Conway, Arkansas.
Death Certificate (state)	Catherine E. Makepeace, death certificate no. A376 (1925), Washington State Board of Health, Olympia.
Deed	John Lancaster to Peter Mitchell, Izard County Deed Book H, page 274, County Clerk's Office, Courthouse, Melbourne, Arkansas.
Electronic Mail (E-mail) Message	Carolyn Earle Billingsley, ''More Dead Folks,'' E-mail message from ceb@rice.edu to Desmond Walls Allen, 31 October 1997.

Source	Footnote Example
Family Group Sheet	Carolyn Earle Billingsley, "John Smith-Sarah Calvert family group sheet," supplied 8 October 1997 by Billingsley to Desmond Walls Allen.
Image File (electronic photograph file)	Photo: James Henry Walls, about 1864, probably Texas County, Missouri. Image file gpawalls.jpg scanned by Rob Walls, 123 Main, Sunnyvale, California, 12 February 1995, from original in his possession.
Interview	Interview with Thurlow Williams, Stone County, Arkansas, by Cuva Williams, 4 July 1977. Transcript prepared by Cuva Williams; copy in possession of Desmond Allen.
Letter	Letter from Alpha Williams, 802 Castaic, Oildale, CA 93308, to Desmond Allen, PO Box 303, Conway, AR 72033, 22 July 1991. Original in possession of Desmond Allen. Miss Williams is the granddaughter of Harrison Williams.
Manuscript	Pence Funeral Home Records, Conway, Arkansas, Book 3, page 87, Pence Collection, Arkansas History Commission, Little Rock.
Marriage Record	Jones-Smith marriage, 17 September 1877, Faulkner County Marriage Book 3, page 72, County Clerk's Office, Conway, Arkansas.
Military Compiled Service Record (microfilmed)	D. H. Grimes, compiled military service record (corporal, Company I, 27th Arkansas Infantry, *Compiled Service Records of Confederate Soldiers Who Served in Organizations from the State of Arkansas*, microfilm publication 317, (Washington, DC: National Archives), roll 195.
Newspaper	"Aged Resident Dies," (Obituary of Jane Smith), *Izard County Register*, Melbourne, Arkansas, 7 August 1947, page 7, column 2.
Pension File	M.C. (Mrs. James) Aaron Confederate pension file, 1904, no. 8,997, "Confederate Pension Applications" microfilmed series, Arkansas History Commission, Little Rock.

Source	Footnote Example
Photograph	Hannah Grimes Moffitt photograph, original, inscribed on back, "Love from your grandma, Hannah Moffitt," date unknown but appears to have been taken during the last years of her life (death was in 1923), photo is 5″×7″. Gift to Desmond Allen in 1988 from Curtis H. Williams, grandson of Hannah Moffitt.
Probate File	Aaron Hightower probate file no. 2478, County Clerk's office, Faulkner County, Arkansas.
Tax Roll (microfilmed)	John Lancaster entry, Izard County 1851 tax list, Blue Mountain township, no pagination, Izard County microfilm roll no. 7, Arkansas History Commission, Little Rock.
Will	James Lingo will (1834), Madison County Will Book 1, page 47, County Clerk's Office, Edwardsville, Illinois.

Appendix B

Resources

This section lists the books and magazines, companies and products mentioned in *First Steps in Genealogy*. It isn't meant as a product endorsement list, just a helpful starting point toward finding the resources and information you need to assist your genealogical research. You'll also find information on government agencies, libraries and genealogical societies.

Addresses for suppliers are included for books that aren't commonly available in bookstores and libraries. If your library doesn't have a particular title, inquire about interlibrary loan. Bookstores can generally special order books they don't routinely stock.

Addresses change. While every effort was made to supply correct, up-to-date addresses, some may be out of date by the time you read this book. Check directories for new information. Web addresses change even more quickly than mailing addresses—use an Internet search engine (Lycos, Alta Vista, Yahoo!, etc.) and enter keywords to find new locations for Web sites. Note that the Web addresses listed below frequently appear to end with a period, but that's just to end a sentence; Web addresses do not conclude with a period.

This section is arranged alphabetically by topic to help you quickly find the references you need.

Adoption

Askin, Jayne and Molly Davis. *Search: A Handbook for Adoptees and Birthparents*. 2nd ed. Phoenix, AZ: Oryx Press, 1992.

Carangelo, Lori. *The Ultimate Search Book: Worldwide Adoption and Vital Records*. 1998 ed. Bountiful, UT. Heritage Quest, 1998.

Paul, Ellen, ed. *The Adoption Directory*. 2nd ed. Detroit: Gale Research, Inc., 1995. [Lists state statutes on adoption, exchanges, agencies, support groups, etc.]

Rillera, Mary Jo. *The Adoption Searchbook: Techniques for Tracing People*. 3rd ed. Westminister, CA: Triadoption Library, Inc., 1991.

Autobiography

Kanin, Ruth. *Write the Story of Your Life*. New York: Hawthorn/Dutton, 1981.

Thomas, Frank P. *How to Write the Story of Your Life*. Cincinnati: Writer's Digest Books, 1989.

Census Records

See "National Archives" below for information on microfilmed census records. Census microfilm catalogs are available online at http://www.nara.gov/.

For unreleased federal census records, contact Personal Service Branch, Bureau of the Census, P.O. Box 1545, Jeffersonville, IN 47131, and ask for the current version of form BC-600.

Census indexes have been published in book form and on CD-ROM by genealogical societies and commercial publishers, notably Accelerated Indexing Systems (books) and Automated Archives (CD-ROM).

Lainhart, Ann S. *State Census Records*. Baltimore: Genealogical Publishing Co., 1992.

Computer Genealogy Programs

There are many excellent genealogy programs on the market. Genealogy magazines (see "Magazines" below) often carry ads and reviews about them. Local genealogical societies frequently have computer interest groups that can supply recommendations about programs. Choose a program that will let you enter a source notation for *each* data item about each person.

Educational Experiences

Federation of Genealogical Societies, P.O. Box 830220, Richardson, TX 75083-0220, hosts an annual conference each year. Write or check the FGS Web site for details: http://www.fgs.org/~fgs/.

National Genealogical Society, 4527 Seventeenth St. N., Arlington, VA 22207, holds an annual conference in cities around the nation. Write or check the NGS web site for details on upcoming events: http://www.genealogy.org/~ngs/.

Repeat Performance, 2911 Crabapple Lane, Hobart, IN 46342, sells audio cassette tapes of lectures on a tremendous variety of topics recorded at national and regional genealogy conferences. Write for a catalog or visit their Web site: http://www.repeatperformance.com/.

Evidence Evaluation

Mills, Elizabeth S. *Evidence! Citation & Analysis for the Family Historian*. Baltimore: Genealogical Publishing Co., Inc., 1997.

Stevenson, Noel C. *Genealogical Evidence: A Guide to the Standard of Proof Relating to Pedigrees, Ancestry, Heirship, and Family History*. Rev. ed., Laguna Hills, CA: Aegean Park Press, 1989.

Forms

Most genealogical vendors (see "Vendors" below) sell forms. Read ads for forms in genealogical magazines (see "Magazines" below). Local Family History Centers in Latter-day Saints (LDS) Churches sell forms at nominal cost.

Dallas Genealogical Society, P.O. Box 12648, Dallas, TX 75225-0648, sells an excellent family group sheet with spaces for source citation of individual data items. For a forms price list, send a SASE. Visit the DGS Web site at http://www.chrysalis.org/dgs.

Everton Publishers, P.O. Box 368, Logan, UT 84323-0368, sells a complete line of supplies and books for genealogists. Write for a catalog or visit their Web site: http://www.everton.com/.

The Genealogy Records Service makes several useful forms available free at its Web site: http://www.genrecords.com.

National Genealogical Society (see "Educational Experiences" above) sells an excellent family group sheet that allows item-level citation notes.

Croom, Emily. *The Unpuzzling Your Past Workbook.* Cincinnati: Betterway Books, 1996.

Dollarhide, William. *Managing a Genealogical Project.* Rev. ed. Baltimore: Genealogical Publishing Co., Inc., 1992, offers forms and a highly structured approach to organization.

Funeral Homes

Several companies publish comprehensive directories of funeral homes in the United States. Your local funeral home's staff will probably let you use their copy of a directory. The Funeral Net Web site at http://www.funeral net.com/ contains a searchable directory of funeral homes and links to other resources.

Handwriting

Kirkham, E. Kay. *How to Read the Handwriting and Records of Early America.* Salt Lake City: Deseret Book Co., 1961. This book is out of print, so look for it in your library or in used bookstores.

Heirlooms

Brackman, Barbara. *Clues in the Calico: A Guide to Identifying and Dating Antique Quilts.* McLean, VA: EPM Publications, Inc., 1989. EPM Publications, P.O. Box 490, McLean, VA 22101.

Groene, Bertram H. *Tracing Your Civil War Ancestor.* 2nd ed. Winston-Salem, NC: John F. Blair Publ., 1996. Helpful in identifying artifacts.

Houses

Light, Sally. *House Histories: A Guide to Tracing the Genealogy of Your Home.* Spencertown, NY: Golden Hill Press, Inc., 1989.

McAlester, Virginia and Lee McAlester. *A Field Guide to American Houses.* New York: Alfred A. Knopf, 1995.

Internet

To locate living people, there are many white-pages directories on the Internet. Some have additional electronic mail address finders, too. Some of them are:

• 411 Directories, http://www.four11.com/

- American Directory Assistance, http://www.lookupusa.com
- Bigfoot, http://www.bigfoot.com
- People Search USA, http://www.infospaceinc.com/people.html
- Switchboard, http://switchboard.com/

Howells, Cyndi. *Netting Your Ancestors: Genealogical Research on the Internet.* Baltimore: Genealogical Publishing Co., Inc., 1997. Cyndi's Internet site, http://www.CyndisList.com is the *best* starting place on the Internet for genealogists.

Renick, Barbara and Richard S. Wilson. *The Internet for Genealogists: A Beginner's Guide,* 3rd ed. La Habra, CA: Compuology, 1997.

Land Records

Hone, E. Wade. *Land & Property Research in the United States.* Salt Lake City: Ancestry, Inc., 1997.

Legal Terms

Black, Henry Campbell. *Black's Law Dictionary: Definitions of the Terms and Phrases of American and English Jurisprudence, Ancient and Modern,* 6th ed. St. Paul, MN: West Publishing Co., 1993. Indispensable reference for understanding cryptic words in old legal documents—the older the book, the better. Look for this book in used bookstores or at going-out-of-business sales of older law firms.

Gifis, Steven H. *Dictionary of Legal Terms: A Simplified Guide to the Language of the Law.* 2nd ed. New York: Barron's Educational Series, Inc., 1993.

Libraries

Most large libraries, including the Library of Congress, have established Web sites on the Internet. To check for a particular library, enter its name in any search engine. To find mailing addresses for libraries, check R.R. Bowker's *American Library Directory* in the reference section of your local library. See also *A Directory of Special Libraries and Information Centers,* published by Gale Research, identifies libraries with especially large genealogy departments.

The **Family History Library,** 35 North West Temple St., Salt Lake City, UT 84150, is the largest genealogical library in the world. You can access many of its holdings by visiting a local Family History Center. To find the location of one, check the library's Web site: http://www.lds.org/Family_History/Where_is.html.

Magazines

Ancestry magazine is published bimonthly by Ancestry, Inc., P.O. Box 476, Salt Lake City, UT 84110-0476. It contains interesting feature articles in a slick, colorful format.

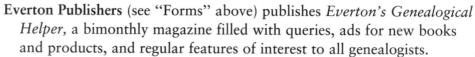

Everton Publishers (see "Forms" above) publishes *Everton's Genealogical Helper,* a bimonthly magazine filled with queries, ads for new books and products, and regular features of interest to all genealogists.

Family Chronicle is published bimonthly and contains articles about all kinds of records. Write *Family Chronicle,* P.O. Box 1201, Lewiston, NY 14092, or check their Web site at http://www.familychronicle.com.

The Family Tree is a tabloid-size newspaper published bimonthly by Odom Library, P.O. Box 1110, Moultrie, GA 31776. It specializes in Scottish clans, but contains information of interest to all. Subscriptions are free, though small postage donations are appreciated.

Heritage Quest Magazine is published bimonthly by Heritage Quest, P.O. Box 329, Bountiful, UT 84011. It contains educational feature articles, regular columns and news of interest. Learn more about it by calling (800) 760-2455.

Maps

The National Archives' Cartographic and Architectural Branch collects a broad range of maps, including census mapping and maps by USGC. Use the Archives' *Special List 29: List of Selected Maps of States and Territories* as a starting point.

Don't neglect the map collections of the Library of Congress; use the Library's online catalog to review map holdings.

Detailed street maps for the entire U.S. are available on the Internet and CD-ROM. You can search an area by zip code, telephone area code or street name.

Tiger Mapping Service at http://tiger.census.gov/instruct.html lets you generate maps online. It's a bit tricky to learn.

United States Geological Survey, 503 National Center, Reston, VA 20192, sells marvelous maps, including topographic maps. Reach them through their Web site: http://www-nmd.usgs.gov/ or call (800) USA-MAPS. The Geographic Names Information System (GNIS) can be searched from the USGS Web site for place names.

Allen, Desmond Walls. *Where to Write for County Maps.* 3rd ed. Conway, AR: Arkansas Research, 1998. $5.95 postpaid reference gives addresses and Web sites for state mapping agencies. Send to Arkansas Research, P.O. Box 303, Conway, AR 72033.

Cobb, David A. *Guide to US Map Resources.* 2nd ed. Chicago: American Library Association, 1990.

The Handy Book for Genealogists, 8th ed. Logan, UT: Everton Publishers, 1991. Contains lists of each state's counties and a county outline map for each state. Also lists county formation data and time frames of available records. See "Forms" above for address.

Jackson, Kenneth T., ed. *Atlas of American History.* 2nd rev. ed. New York: Charles Scribner's Sons, 1984. There are several books with this title; search for this particular one as it's excellent.

Makower, Joel, ed. *The Map Catalog,* 3rd ed. New York: Vintage Books, 1992. Wonderful descriptive material and illustrations of all kinds of maps.

Sale, Randall D. and Edwin D. Karn. *American Expansion: A Book of Maps.* Lincoln, Neb.: University of Nebraska Press, Reprint, 1979. This thin volume shows settlement patterns and public land offices.

Thorndale, William and William Dollarhide. *Map Guide to the US Federal Censuses, 1790–1920.* Baltimore: Genealogical Publishing Co., Reprint, 1992. Absolutely essential for serious researchers; a must for census work.

Medical Considerations

Krause, Carol. *How Healthy Is Your Family Tree?: A Complete Guide to Tracing Your Family's Medical and Behavioral History.* Old Tappan, N.J.: Macmillan Publishing Co., Inc., 1995.

Methodology Guides

Repeat Performance (see "Educational Experiences" above) sells audio cassette tapes of how-to genealogy lectures presented at conferences.

Allen, Desmond Walls and Carolyn Earle Billingsley. *Beginner's Guide to Family History Research.* 3rd ed. Conway, AR: Arkansas Research, 1997. P.O. Box 303, Conway, AR 72033.

Croom, Emily Anne, *The Genealogist's Companion and Sourcebook.* Cincinnati: Betterway Books, 1994.

Croom, Emily Anne. *Unpuzzling Your Past.* 3rd ed. Cincinnati: Betterway Books, 1995.

Greenwood, Val D. *The Researcher's Guide to American Genealogy.* 2nd ed. Baltimore: Genealogical Publishing Co., Inc., 1990.

Rubincam, Milton. *Pitfalls in Genealogical Research.* 2nd ed. Salt Lake City: Ancestry, Inc., Reprint, 1987.

Szucs, Loretto Dennis and Sandra Hargreaves Luebking, eds. *The Source: A Guidebook of American Genealogy,* revised ed. Salt Lake City: Ancestry, Inc., 1997. A marvelous reference book for all aspects of genealogy.

Microfilm Rental

Genealogical magazines (see "Magazines" above) carry ads for several rental programs.

AGLL/Heritage Quest, P.O. Box 329, Bountiful, UT 84011, has a membership program for microfilm rentals. Write for information or check their Web site at http://www.heritagequest.com.

Military Records

Records for volunteer soldiers called into service for twentieth-century wars are housed at the National Personnel Records Center, 9700 Page

Blvd., St. Louis, MO 63132. Some of the records were lost in a fire in 1973. Request the current version of Standard Form 180 to order copies of documents.

Military records from pre-twentieth-century wars are housed at the National Archives (see "National Archives" below) in Washington, DC. Request Form NATF-80 to submit requests.

Neagles, James C. *US Military Records: A Guide to Federal and State Sources from Colonial Times to the Present.* Salt Lake City: Ancestry, Inc., 1994.

Oberly, James W. *Sixty Million Acres: American Veterans and the Public Lands Before the Civil War.* Kent, OH: Kent State University Press, 1990.

National Archives

The National Archives, Washington, DC 20408, houses a tremendous collection of records of interest to genealogists. For current information about locations and phone numbers, check their Web site at http://www .nara.gov.

The complete text for the latest guide to the National Archives and all their microfilm catalogs are available online. See also: *Guide to Genealogical Research in the National Archives.* Washington, DC: National Archives Trust Fund Board, 1985.

Regional branches of the National Archives include:
- National Archives—Alaska Region, 654 W. Third Ave., Anchorage, AK 99501-2154
- National Archives—Central Plains Region, 2312 E. Bannister Rd., Kansas City, MO 64131-3011
- National Archives—Great Lakes Region, 7358 S. Pulaski Rd., Chicago, IL 60629-5898
- National Archives—Mid-Atlantic Region, 900 Market St., Philadelphia, PA 19107-4292
- National Archives—Northeast Region, Frederick C. Murphy Federal Center, 380 Trapelo Rd., Waltham, MA 02154-6399
- National Archives—Northeast Region, 201 Varick St., New York, NY 10014-4811
- National Archives—Pacific Alaska Region, 6125 Sand Point Way NE, Seattle, WA 98115-7999
- National Archives—Pacific Region, 1000 Commodore Dr., San Bruno, CA 94066-2350
- National Archives—Pacific Region, 24000 Avila Rd., Laguna Niguel, CA 92677-3497 (P.O. Box 6719, 92607-6719)
- National Archives—Rocky Mountain Region, Bldg. 48, Denver Federal Center, Denver, CO 80225

- National Archives—Southeast Region, 1557 St. Joseph Ave., East Point, GA 30344
- National Archives—Southwest Region, 501 Felix St., Ft. Worth, TX 76115

Oral History

Chapin, Alice. *Reaching Back*. Cincinnati: Betterway Books, 1997.

Davis, Cullom, and others. *Oral History: From Tape to Type*. Reprint, Ann Arbor, MI: Books on Demand. (Books on Demand photocopies old out-of-print books.)

Shumway, Gary L. and William G. Hartley. *An Oral History Primer*. Salt Lake City: Primer Publications, 1983.

Photographs

Shull, Wilma Sadler. *Photographing Your Heritage*. Salt Lake City: Ancestry, Inc., 1988.

Weinstein, Robert A., and Larry Booth. *Collection, Use, and Care of Historical Photographs*. Nashville: American Association for State and Local History, 1989.

Preservation of Documents

Gaylord Brothers, Inc., P.O. Box 4901, Syracuse, NY 13221, is a library supplier with a line of archivally safe boxes, folders, cleaning supplies, plastic paper clips and Abbey pH Pens to test for acid content in paper. Visit their Web site at http://www.gaylord.com or use your local librarian's copy of their catalog.

Light Impressions, P.O. Box 940, Rochester, NY 14603, carries all kinds of archival supplies. Their albums, scrapbooks and photo storage systems are especially helpful to genealogists. Request a free catalog from (800) 828-6216.

Publishing a Family History

Hatcher, Patricia Law. *Producing a Quality Family History*. Salt Lake City: Ancestry, Inc., 1996. *Everything* you need to know about the subject.

Polking, Kirk. *Writing Family Histories and Memoirs*. Cincinnati: Betterway Books, 1995.

Ross, Tom and Marilyn. *The Complete Guide to Self-Publishing*, 3rd ed. Cincinnati: Writer's Digest Books, 1994.

Research Trips

Warren, Paula Stuart and James W. Warren. *Getting the Most Mileage from Genealogical Research Trips*. 3rd ed. St. Paul, MN: Warren Research and Publishing, 1998. Wonderful advice from the experts on this topic.

Warren, Paula Stuart and James W. Warren. *Making the Most of Your*

Research Trip to Salt Lake City. 6th ed. St. Paul, MN: Warren Research and Publishing, 1997. Order from the publisher at 1869 Laurel Ave., St. Paul, MN 55104.

Reunions
Ninkovich, Thomas and Barbara E. Brown. *The Family Reunion Handbook.* San Francisco: Reunion Research, 1992.

Self-Directed Learning
Gross, Ronald. *The Independent Scholar's Handbook.* Berkeley, CA: Ten Speed Press, 1993. Applicable to any subject.

Gross, Ronald. *Peak Learning: A Master Course in Learning How to Learn.* Los Angeles: Jeremy P. Tarcher, Inc., 1991.

Social History
There are thousands of titles that could be listed in this section; the following volumes are only a few examples. For more information about searching for information on specific topics, see Francis Paul Prucha's *Handbook for Research in American History: A Guide to Bibliographies and Other Reference Works.* 2nd ed., revised. Lincoln: University of Nebraska Press, 1994.

Billington, Ray Allen. *Westward Expansion: A History of the American Frontier.* New York: The Macmillan Co., 1982. This volume has been through several editions—check libraries and used bookstores.

Boorstin, Daniel J. *The Americans: The Colonial Experience.* New York: Random House, 1958. Paperback editions are still in print.

Boorstin, Daniel J. *The Americans: The Democratic Experience.* New York: Random House, 1973. Paperback editions are still in print.

Boorstin, Daniel J. *The Americans: The National Experience.* New York: Random House, 1965. [paperback editions are still in print]

Crissman, James K. *Death and Dying in Central Appalachia: Changing Attitudes and Practices.* Urbana: University of Illinois Press, 1994.

Fischer, David Hackett. *Albion's Seed: Four British Folkways in America.* New York: Oxford University Press, 1989. (Also available in paperback, 1991.)

Friedman, Lawrence M. *A History of American Law.* Rev. ed. New York: Simon and Schuster, 1986.

Habenstein, Robert W. and William M. Lamers. *The History of American Funeral Directing.* Milwaukee, WI: Bulfin Printers, Inc., 1963.

Hawke, David Freeman. *Everyday Life in Early America.* New York: HarperCollins, 1989.

Hughes, Kristine. *The Writer's Guide to Everyday Life in Regency and Victorian England.* Cincinnati: Writer's Digest Books, 1998.

Leyburn, James G. *The Scotch-Irish: A Social History.* Reprint. Chapel Hill: University of North Carolina Press, 1989.

McCutcheon, Marc. *The Writer's Guide to Everyday Life From Prohibition Through World War II*. Cincinnati: Writer's Digest Books, 1995.

McCutcheon, Marc. *The Writer's Guide to Everyday Life in the 1800s*. Cincinnati: Writer's Digest Books, 1993.

McWhiney, Grady. *Cracker Culture: Celtic Ways in the Old South*. Tuscaloosa, AL: The University of Alabama Press, 1988.

Morgan, Ted. *A Shovel of Stars: The Making of the American West, 1800 to the Present*. New York: Simon and Schuster, 1995.

Morgan, Ted. *Wilderness at Dawn: The Settling of the North American Continent*. New York: Simon and Schuster, 1993. (Also available in paperback, 1994.)

Ramsey, Robert W. *Carolina Cradle: Settlement of the Northwest Carolina Frontier, 1747–1762*. Reprint. Chapel Hill: University of North Carolina Press, 1987.

Riley, Glenda. *Divorce: An American Tradition*. New York: Oxford University Press, 1991.

Shammas, Carole, Marylynn Salmon and Michel Dahlin. *Inheritance in America: From Colonial Times to the Present*. Galveston, TX: Frontier Press, 1997.

Sloane, David Charles. *The Last Great Necessity: Cemeteries in American History*. Baltimore: The Johns Hopkins University Press, 1991. (Also available in paperback, 1995.)

Sowell, Thomas. *Ethnic America: A History*. New York: Basic Books, 1983. Especially relevant for the Irish, German, Jewish, Italian, Chinese, Japanese, African-American, Puerto Ricans and Mexican researcher.

Taylor, Dale. *The Writer's Guide to Everyday Life in Colonial America*. Cincinnati: Writer's Digest Books, 1997.

Social Security Administration

Social Security Administration, Freedom of Information Office, 4-H-8 Annex Bldg., 6401 Security Blvd., Baltimore, MD 21235, can supply (for a fee) a copy of the SS-5 form for a deceased person or that of a living person, provided permission is given. For details about Social Security's services to genealogists, request *Social Security: A Genealogical Resource* from Arkansas Research, P.O. Box 303, Conway, AR 72033 ($5.95 postpaid).

Societies

Use an Internet search engine to seek Web sites for genealogical societies. Check the US GenWeb project at http://www.netins.net/showcase /pafways/genweb.htm for the location of interest.

The Federation of Genealogical Societies (see "Educational Experiences" above) publishes a directory of member societies and offers a comprehensive list of societies on its Web site.

Your local library may have a copy of Elizabeth Petty Bentley's *The Genealogist's Address Book*, and historical societies and museums are included with genealogical society listings in a directory published by the American Association for State and Local History.

Smith, Juliana. *Ancestry's Address Book: A Comprehensive List of Local, State, and Federal Agencies and Institutions.* Salt Lake City: Ancestry, Inc., 1997.

Source Citation
The Chicago Manual of Style. 14th ed. Chicago: University of Chicago Press, 1993.

Mills, Elizabeth S. *Evidence! Citation & Analysis for the Family Historian.* Baltimore: Genealogical Publishing Co., Inc., 1997.

Vendors
Learn about the wonderful variety of books, forms and services by reading ads in genealogical magazines (see "Magazines" above), and browse the used bookstores in your area for out-of-print titles and (often) lower prices.

AGLL/Heritage Quest (see "Microfilm Rental" above) supplies everything from preservation materials to forms, books and microfilm.

Amazon Books, http://www.amazon.com, supplies all kinds of books through an online catalog.

Ancestry, Inc. (see "Magazines" above) publishes very good resource books for genealogists. Their Web site (http://www.ancestry.com/) offers searchable databases.

Broderbund, P.O. Box 6125, Novato, CA 94948, sells genealogical software and CD-ROMs containing a massive amount of data. Their World Family Tree series contains millions of ancestor submissions from all over the world. Write for a catalog or log onto their Web site at http://www.familytreemaker.com.

Everton Publishers (see "Forms" above) sells a wide variety of genealogical supplies.

Genealogical Publishing Co., Inc., 1001 N. Calvert St., Baltimore, MD 21202, http://www.genealogical.com/, publishes books about every genealogical topic.

Hearthstone Bookshop, 5735-A Telegraph Rd., Alexandria, VA 22303, sells a variety of books from many publishers. Visit them online at http://www.hearthstonebooks.com/.

Vital Records
Kemp, Thomas J. *International Vital Records Handbook.* 3rd ed. Baltimore: Genealogical Publishing Co., Inc., 1994.

National Center for Health Statistics Staff. Edit. Klaudia Cox. *Where to Write for Vital Records: Births, Deaths, Marriages, and Divorces.*

Hyattsville, MD: National Center for Health Statistics. Order the latest edition from Superintendent of Documents, Government Printing Office Washington, DC 20402.

Addresses and price lists for obtaining vital records from courthouses and other repositories can be found on the Internet at http://www.vitalchek .com.

Call the Social Security Administration's toll-free number (listed under United States Government in telephone directories) to inquire about addresses, fees, etc. of state vital records offices.

Writing Skills

Brusaw, Charles T., Gerald J. Alred, and Walter E. Oliu. *The Business Writer's Handbook*. 4th rev. ed. New York: St. Martin's Press, 1993. Also published as *Handbook of Technical Writing 5* (1997). Presents five steps to successful writing: preparation, research, organization, writing and revision.

Cheney, Theodore A. Rees. *Getting the Words Right*. Cincinnati: Writer's Digest Books, 1990.

Cook, Claire Kehrwald. *The MLA's Line by Line: How to Edit Your Own Writing*. Boston: Houghton Mifflin Co., 1985. Advice from an editor on "loose, baggy sentences, faulty connections, ill-matched partners" and other writing problems.

Fiske, Robert Hartwell. *The Writer's Digest Dictionary of Concise Writing*. Cincinnati: Writer's Digest Books, 1996.

Fryxell, David. *Structure and Flow*. Cincinnati: Writer's Digest Books, 1996.

Lederer, Richard and Richard Dowis. *The Write Way: The S.P.E.L.L.* * *Guide to Real-Life Writing*. New York: Pocket Books, 1995. *Society for the Preservation of English Language and Literature; humorous approach.

Sabin, William A. *The Gregg Reference Manual*. 8th ed. New York: Glencoe McGraw-Hill Co., 1996.

Stilman, Anne. *Grammatically Correct: The Writer's Guide to Punctuation, Spelling, Style, Usage and Grammar*. Cincinnati: Writer's Digest Books, 1997.

Zinsser, William. *On Writing Well: An Informal Guide to Writing Nonfiction*. 5th ed. San Bernardino, CA: Borgo Press, 1996.

Index

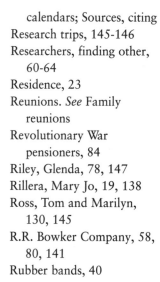